Nothing Impossible

Memoirs of a United States Cavalryman In World War 2

Wallace L. Clement

Edited by Sean M. Heuvel

MERRIAM PRESS

HOOSICK FALLS NEW YORK

2017

First published in 2017 by the Merriam Press

First Edition

ISBN 9781576386316
Library of Congress Control Number: 2017910518

This work was designed, produced, and published in
the United States of America by the

Merriam Press
489 South Street
Hoosick Falls NY 12090

E-mail: ray@merriam-press.com
Web site: merriam-press.com

The Merriam Press publishes new manuscripts on historical subjects, especially military history and with an emphasis on World War II, as well as reprinting previously published works, including reports, documents, manuals, articles and other materials on historical topics.

Dedication

Pfc. Dallas C. Anderson
Sgt. Roscoe J. Browning
S/Sgt. Thomas R. Carnes
Pfc. John C. Carr, Jr.
Pvt. Bill D. Curtis
Pfc. Oliverio Dorrance
Pfc. Porfirio J. Escobar
Sgt. Richard T. Esslinger
Pvt. John R. Gallitano
Sgt. Ney C. Galway
2nd Lt. Wilson E. Gwyn
Sgt. Alexander Harmon
Cpl. Vincent B. Hernandez, Jr.

Pvt. Roy M. Johnson
Sgt. Charles H. Lindsey
Pvt. Tranquilino Martinez
T/5 George E. McCollough
2nd Lt. Carl Mueller, Jr.
Cpl. W.A. Nelson
T/4 Albert J. Pine
Pvt. Vincent H. Schanhaar
1st Lt. Jacob Schnell
Sgt. Wayne W. Showalter
Sgt. James R. Slater
Cpl. Harold White
Pfc. Alfred C. Widener
1st Lt. James D. Yurk

To these men of the 804th Tank Destroyer Battalion who gave the ultimate in sacrifice, we dedicate this book. May we face the future as bravely and unselfishly as they faced the enemy, remembering always the outstanding example of patriotism and devotion to duty which was theirs.

Wallace L. Clement
Major, Cavalry,
Commanding

Contents

Capt. Wallace L. Clement in Northern Ireland – Fall 1942 (Clement Family Collection).

Brig. Gen. Wallace L. Clement – circa 1968 (U.S. Army Photograph).

Foreword

THE day my father passed away, I was hundreds of miles away hiking in the Smoky Mountains near Gatlinburg, Tennessee. My sister spent most of the day trying to reach me on the telephone and finally succeeded in the late afternoon. Stunned by the sad news, I began my trip back home to collect my uniform along with some necessary items for the trip that I was about to take. Driving on to Williamsburg, Virginia, with my wife and daughter accompanying me, I had plenty of time to reflect on who my father was, not only as my Dad, but also as a proven military leader who had been in action many times during his 30 years and three wars. I delivered the eulogy at his Memorial Mass in Williamsburg. Speaking extemporaneously, having focused on just a few main themes, I was told afterwards by one of his West Point classmates who had been in attendance that my comments had touched him greatly. Apparently, I had been able to eulogize my Dad as I also related the complexities of my relationship with him as his son. Having made no notes then, and with nothing preserved except in my memory, I will now try to relate the substance of what I was thinking about when I made those remarks. Allow me to travel back in my mind to the summer of 2000 when I spoke, Dad having died a little over a year before 9/11.

Even as a boy, I appreciated the fact that Dad had been recognized by our nation as a hero in the truest sense of the word. I knew that he had been decorated with the Distinguished Service Cross, Silver Star Medal and the Bronze Star Medal with "V" for Valor. However, most details of the events that resulted in these decorations were largely unknown to me until I was older. For example, Dad had related to all of us as kids about how he had been captured by the Germans in Italy. However, only years later did I realize that the combat action cited in his Distinguished Service Cross citation had ended with him being listed as Missing in Action (MIA). His mother was so notified by telegram. As you will read, he was not MIA. Regaining consciousness in a ditch after surviving a jeep crash when his brave driver had been shot out of the vehicle and died, Dad was captured. Up to the moment of the crash, he had zealously and bravely continued his efforts to influence the outcome of that battle with the Germans.

This book ends with Dad's service in Korea, making reference to his later assignments and awards. I remember when he won the Silver Star Medal in Vietnam. His gallantry in action included him ordering his command (division-level then as ADC) helicopter to land in a hot LZ (translation—active battle raging below) where he assisted in loading several wounded soldiers aboard—a "dust off" operation as he termed it. This was just another example of him doing his duty in his eyes, nothing more. I was old enough to understand what he had done some thousands of miles away from home, even though my mother was mortified having already learned of the deaths of other Army generals in helicopter crashes over there. I knew also that he would have done it again, and that he would have expected any soldier to do the same. I like to think that I would have.

I have three older sisters (Sarah, Ellen, and Anne) and a twin brother (Doug) who is older by 15 minutes. That 15 minutes is a big deal in my family as they constantly remind me that I am the baby of the family. Being the youngest of five children brought on much of what one would expect for me to experience growing up. My Dad demanded excellence from us all. For me, a good report card usually meant being asked about a sole "B" mark with no praise or comment about all the "A" marks noted alongside it. Chuckling about this now, I grew to understand that this was just how Dad drove himself and those he loved. To be the son of my father meant that I was raised in a spirit of "no quarter asked, none given." Some of his favorite guiding principles were voiced as comments made to me. Many were in reference to the great Confederate General during our Civil War, Stonewall Jackson. "Never take counsel of your fears"; "There stands Jackson like a stone wall! Rally around the Virginian!" and others flood my memory now as I write. If I became too effusive in praise about a schoolmate, Dad would remind me that "neither is your blood ditchwater" (in reference to Napoleon's famous quote). I suppose that he wanted me to "keep battlin" (another favorite expression) and not lessen my efforts to win even in the face of good competition. This was true in sports as well—he loved taking my brother and me to our Little League baseball games and practices. He taught us to play "Pepper" and "Home Run"—batting back into the backstop to learn hitting accuracy. Indeed, Dad was photographed in baseball action shots and included in a book entitled *Sports as Taught and Played at West Point*. This book was published in the late '30's or early '40's. Rumor has it that a surviving volume of this book somehow appeared in his collection late in life after a reunion trip to West Point. You will read that Dad was an intercollegiate boxing champion while at West Point. If he ever caught my brother and me fighting he would order "Gloves on!" and make us punch each other to exhaustion—giving us good pointers for jab and defense throughout! "Keep those hands up mister!"

Dad raised us to tell the entire truth, never, ever, "waffle," and to state "no excuse, sir" instead of some half-baked explanation for a fault discovered and brought in full scrutiny before his demanding visage. I readily adapted to a childhood of avoiding such encounters altogether with my father, however and whenever possible. I somehow believe now that I got the worst of this out of "we five," perhaps because Dad recognized that I might wish to be a young lieutenant someday. It should go without saying that he would certainly not have wanted any of his children to be found wanting as were Lieutenants A, B and C in this book. Nevertheless, I then counted as a good week one in which I had no such encounters. However, I learned that "no excuse" brought an unavoidable encounter to a much speedier and satisfactory conclusion for me rather than showing fear and weakness by mouthing out whatever came to mind in the typical fashion of dumb kids everywhere! Much as Dad remarks upon in the Epilogue, I share his belief that the youth of today would be far better served by being raised and educated with this and similar principles utilized. Molding young folks into fine citizens with a well-grounded respect for the things that matter is not a passive activity. Dad was living and active proof of that in my life as I grew from a boy into a man.

As you will see in the pages that follow, Dad loved to read. He instilled that love in all of us. My brilliant oldest sister Sarah displays that love and respect for the written word very well indeed. Ours was a family that celebrated Thanksgiving not only by eating a grand meal, but also by passing well-worn books around to read passages aloud. Rudyard Kipling was a favorite of his and even now I can hear "Gunga Din" and "Tommy" being read out loud in full voice, with appropriate inflections added. Dad also loved the works of Robert Frost and many others. He grew up reading what we today call "the great books," and his fine collection survives him largely in the home library at Sarah's house. I have his military books including those few he could pack along with him all through the war in Africa and Europe and later in other wars. I remain ever grateful to have had access to such a wonderful collection to read and reflect upon as I served my own military career—not quite following in my father's footsteps.

Not quite? In the summer of 1977, I declined a last-minute appointment to the U.S. Air Force Academy because I had by then come to understand that my poor eyesight and defective color vision would keep me out of any military airplane cockpit. I elected instead to accept the admission offer extended to me by the University of Virginia. It took Dad awhile to come to peace with my decision. However, Mom and my siblings were all for it. With regard to my own career serving in the U.S. Marine Corps, obviously my Dad was thrilled about the decision I made in my second year "on the grounds" to go that route by joining the Naval ROTC program. Dad was even more thrilled when I told him that I had won a Naval ROTC scholarship for my third and fourth years at UVA. With my twin brother already enlisted and serving in the Marines, I was drawn to the Corps as well. Dad remarked that he had no problems with us joining the Marines in the late '70's and early '80's as "today's Marine Corps reminds (me) of (my) Army of the 1940's" He did not see why I wanted to go to Airborne School and jump out of perfectly good airplanes. Nonetheless, he exclaimed pride in "the silver wings upon my chest" when I returned from Fort Benning, Georgia over the summer of 1980. While at Fort Benning, I had been able to visit with his old friend and comrade in arms, Col. Mike Tully, who was then the commander of The School Brigade—the parent unit for all of the schools there.

Even during my tenure as a company-grade officer, during which time I had deployed twice to Beirut, Lebanon, served in Grenada, led a boat raid into the sea port of Mogadishu, Somalia, and sailed in the Persian Gulf afterwards, Dad did not address his wartime exploits with me in great detail. It was when I was selected to command an infantry battalion in the reserve component that Dad looked me in the eye with pride to say that "now, at last, you will be in a position to really affect a lot of young lives. Rise to the challenge and make a difference in your and their battlespace. You will not be judged by how you handle things when they are going well. No, you will be judged by how you handle a crisis, when things are falling apart all around you." These heart-felt words were delivered as he rested in a hospital bed after a heart procedure. We both teared up a bit. Passion and emotion run just under the surface for us Clements. He only had months to live but we didn't know that then. He was gone before I assumed command of that battalion.

NOTHING IMPOSSIBLE

Except in my thoughts, he was not there for me to discuss my later service in Baghdad with ORHA/CPA, my orders to take my family to France for a year as the first-ever liaison officer to the French Marines, my selection to attend and my graduation from the U.S. Army War College, and my service as Deputy Chief of Staff, Marine Forces Europe. While my brother was able to join me for my retirement dinner and ceremony in San Francisco, California, Dad obviously was not, even though he had enjoyed several stays at the Marines Memorial Club where we had this dinner. My CG remarked that I had "never missed a school or a war." When he handed over the podium for me to speak, Dad was on my mind a great deal that night as I gave my remarks to the assembled officers of the Division. I was retired with 30 years of service having served the last two years as the ADC of the 4th Marine Division. I was proud to have served at the last in a Brigadier General's billet: the same billet my Dad had in Vietnam. His memory is strong within me even today and I continue to perceive the wisdom and truth of his guiding principles, harsh as they may seem to what he would certainly see as a coddled and pampered U.S.A. of today. I recall saying that with my father now gone, I had no regrets for anything left unsaid between us. I counted that fact then, and now, as a true blessing. Yes, later in Dad's life, he and I discussed our father-son relationship in detail. He opened up quite a bit with me—perhaps more so than with my siblings—and I came to know that he did the best he knew and could. I am so grateful to him today for that.

At the constant urging of "we five" children, Dad finally began late in life to put pen to paper and record his memoirs for us. The book before you is a direct result of Dad's efforts. However, it would not have come into being in this form without the initiative and leadership of Dr. Sean Heuvel, to whom "we five" and Dad's family will continue to feel indebted in this regard. As a young boy then, Dr. Heuvel came to know my father as Dad's young neighbor late in Dad's life. They struck up a friendship and a mentor relationship. Knowing how much my father appreciated intelligent discourse, I am sure that the two shared hours of good conversation about leadership and making a difference to those around you in life. I am honored that Dr. Heuvel sought to do the work necessary to have my father's words published. While there are many books and stories published about heroism, leadership, and military history, only this book is about my father. I most appreciate your taking the time to read it. I believe that you will find the time in reading well spent, as my Dad's life and his career in the United States Army are most worthy of comment and emulation. Enjoy the read, God Bless you all...and success to the Marines!

—Col. David J. Clement, USMCR (Ret.)
Munfordville, Kentucky
June 2016

Preface

AS a young teenager growing up in Williamsburg, Virginia, I lived down the street from a most interesting man who I knew at the time as "Mr. Clement." I will therefore refer to him as such in the Preface and Introduction to this book. Mr. Clement was an active retiree who enjoyed among other pastimes working part-time as a historic interpreter for the Colonial Williamsburg Foundation. As I recall, my parents first met Mr. Clement and his wife Joan at a neighborhood function—sometime around the mid-1990s. A short time later, a school assignment pertaining to World War II history prompted my Mother to recommend my getting in touch with Mr. Clement, as she knew that he was a veteran of that conflict. A friendship quickly ensued between Mr. Clement and me, and he was most gracious in offering guidance, camaraderie, and wisdom to an impressionable and naïve young man.

I recall spending many afternoons in the Clements' den immersed in conversation with Mr. Clement. I would talk about my post-high school plans and professional aspirations while he would talk about his children, grandchildren and some of his own life experiences. However, most of the time our conversations centered on our mutual love for history—particularly the World War II era. A master storyteller, Mr. Clement often regaled me with accounts of his time spent in North Africa and Italy. I in turn was fascinated to hear these stories directly from someone who was there, and especially someone who was in the presence of such World War II luminaries as Generals George S. Patton and Mark Clark. Interestingly, while Mr. Clement spoke in great detail about certain aspects of his service in World War II and later conflicts, he never discussed his rank nor any awards or honors that he earned. I therefore came to believe that he likely served in an honorable yet uneventful manner during the course of his Army service. Boy was I wrong!

One can imagine my shock when I one day asked Mr. Clement what rank he held when he left the Army. I fully expected him to say that he retired as a sergeant or something. Instead, he mentioned in a most unassuming manner, "Oh, I retired as a brigadier general. I was an assistant division commander in Vietnam and had my own staff, my own command helicopter, etc." All these years later, I still remember my jaw hitting the ground when I heard Mr. Clement say that. Moreover, it was not until years after his passing when I had direct access to his military records that I began to understand the full picture concerning GENERAL Clement's military service. This was a man who saw extensive combat in not just one but THREE wars—World War II, Korea, and Vietnam. Further, Mr. Clement had earned every major U.S. Army combat decoration short of the Medal of Honor. These included the Distinguished Service Cross, the Silver Star, the Bronze Star, the Distinguished Flying Cross, and a host of others. I was further surprised to discover that Mr. Clement had been a POW during the final stages of World War II and had survived the experience. He had mentioned none of this to me during our many conversations. Today, it reminds me of the famous Margaret Thatcher quote, "being powerful is like being a lady—if you have to say you are; you are not." Mr. Clement knew who he was and felt no need to advertise his many accolades to others. In Mr. Clement's mind, he had just been doing his duty as a West Point-trained U.S. Army officer—nothing more. This presented me with a powerful lesson in humility and leadership that I carry with me to this day.

A few years later, I learned of Mr. Clement's passing when I was a sophomore in college, and while our conversations ceased, his guidance and example always remained in the back of my mind. As the years passed, I graduated from college, earned master's degrees and a doctorate, and became an academic while starting my own family. While pursuing various book projects on U.S. military history, I began to think increasingly about Mr. Clement and the vague recollections I had about his writing memoirs that explored his own World War II experiences. Wouldn't it be neat, I thought, if I could help finish the literary journey that he began and make those memoirs available to the public at large? I therefore began to reach out to Mr. Clement's widow Joan, his children, and his step-children—a full 15 years after Mr. Clement's passing—and they responded with an outpouring of interest and enthusiasm. They were also most kind in sharing with me all of Mr. Clement's writings, wartime photos, service records, and other related materials. As I began to study those materials, it only reinforced my belief

NOTHING IMPOSSIBLE

that Mr. Clement's World War II memoirs should be formally published. Along with it being a fascinating historical account, I quickly realized that the memoirs were also essentially a textbook about leadership that could be of immense use in a classroom environment. This book is a culmination of this process of thought, research, and intention.

Ultimately, my motivation to edit and annotate Mr. Clement's World War II memoirs was largely personal. I thought it would be a fitting way to say THANK YOU for the role that he played in my life all of those years ago. Further, I thought a book of this nature would be a fitting tribute to a man who devoted 30 years of his life to the service of this country while asking for very little in return. Most importantly, I believed that it was crucial to highlight the heroism and sacrifice of U.S. Military personnel who served on the Italian Front during World War II—a theater of the war that is sometimes overshadowed by other legendary battles and campaigns, such as D-Day and the Battle of the Bulge, that were fought elsewhere in western Europe. This was certainly a point of contention with Mr. Clement, who believed that the soldiers under his command deserved better when it came to U.S. media attention during the period. Overall, I hope that this book fascinates and inspires future generations of readers in the same way that it has impacted me. It is important that these stories of duty, sacrifice, and heroism be preserved for future generations.

Introduction

Wallace L. Clement's life reads like the lives of several men combined. After an active childhood in the Boston area, he graduated from West Point in 1940 and went on to perform distinguished combat service in three different wars—World War II, Korea, and Vietnam. As mentioned in the Preface, Mr. Clement earned a wide range of U.S. Army decorations and reached the rank of brigadier general before retiring in 1970. Along the way, he married, raised five children, and played an important role in the lives of his two stepchildren and multiple grandchildren. Mr. Clement also had a productive post-Army career working for various military think tanks and later pursued his love of history in retirement as an interpreter for the Colonial Williamsburg Foundation. His was a life well lived.

During his final years and at the urging of his children, Mr. Clement went to work writing his military memoirs. He wrote extensively about his World War II service, and had plans to do the same for his service in the Korean War and Vietnam. However, declining health prompted by a history of heart problems—the same ailment that conspired to block his promotion to major general and facilitate his Army retirement—did not make that endeavor entirely possible. However, Mr. Clement put an enormous amount of effort into drafting his World War II reminiscences. I discovered this first-hand while doing background research for this book. Among his papers were hundreds of pages of writing, notes, original photographs, and other related materials. It was clear that he wanted his story told—not so much to commemorate his own service, but to help future generations understand the enormous effort and sacrifice put forth by U.S. Army personnel in the war's Italian Campaign. As mentioned in the Preface, Mr. Clement always believed that this theater of the war was overlooked by the media and public at large, and I believe that he set out to write his memoirs in order to help correct that.

In turn, this book is intended to complete the work that Mr. Clement began so many years ago. As editor, my task was to organize and annotate all of his original writings into a single flowing, comprehensible manuscript. As I studied his papers, I discovered that Mr. Clement wrote his World War II memoirs over a period of several years—mostly in the 1990s. However, there were also relevant reflective writings that he drafted as far back as 1945. I therefore organized these disparate reminiscences into a single manuscript, and endeavored to use Mr. Clement's original words as much as possible. In some sections, I had to take a bit of artistic license to draft transition sentences that would effectively link together separate bodies of writing that were likely written at different times. In these cases, I did my best to write in Mr. Clement's tone. Further, once organized into individual chapters, I annotated all of Mr. Clement's writing and created footnotes in order to provide context and elaboration for modern readers. I also included a range of photographs, maps, and other images—many of which were from Mr. Clement's papers—to help provide greater depth to his story.

As readers will note, the chapters unfold in a chronological manner. Chapters One and Two explore Mr. Clement's childhood in Cambridge and Boston, as well as his time as a cadet at West Point and his early cavalry service in California. Chapter Three covers his move to the 804th Tank Destroyer Battalion and subsequent training and service in the United States, the United Kingdom, and North Africa. Chapters Four, Five, and Six examine Mr. Clement's service in Italy as the 804th TDB's executive officer and include a harrowing account of his time as a prisoner of war under the Germans. Except for Chapter Three, all of these early chapters are largely Mr. Clement's own original writing. As he did not write much about his time training in the United Kingdom and North Africa, I had to utilize other sources to fill that gap. These included a battalion history that he co-wrote in 1945 as well as the post-war memoirs of a soldier—Sgt. Reed Van Wagenen—who served under his command. Chapter Seven consists of the leadership lessons that Mr. Clement learned from his World War II experiences. This chapter stemmed from a military monograph that he wrote as a student in an advanced officer class at the Armored School at Fort Knox in 1948. It was originally entitled "Some Personal Observations," and covered the personal observations he accumulated from his wartime service as well as the specific lessons that he learned about doing the impossible (hence the title of this book), being ready for the unex-

NOTHING IMPOSSIBLE

pected, and judging the character of subordinates quickly and correctly as an officer.

The Epilogue explores Mr. Clement's Korean War service and briefly discusses his later Army career and retirement. This chapter was based on an essay he wrote about his Korean War experience as well as some small snippets of writing about his later life. Toward the end of the chapter, I had to include some transition sentences using Mr. Clement's tone to bring it all to a close. In order to provide additional historical context, I also included extensive appendices in this book. Included are sections that list his dates of rank and decorations, the MIA telegram that the Army sent to his Mother in May 1945, and the list of enemy equipment and personnel captured by the 804th Tank Destroyer Battalion during World War II. Also included in the appendices is a July 2001 letter from 804th veteran Morris Snow that provides reminiscences about Mr. Clement, and finally some highlights (written in fall 1945) of the 804th's service in North Africa and Europe.

Editing and annotating memoirs is not a simple endeavor, and it takes a significant number of people to help bring the task to a successful conclusion. I was fortunate to have the able assistance of a number of individuals in completing this book. First, I must thank Mr. Clement's widow, Joan Clement, for making his body of World War II-related writing available for publication. Her enthusiasm and support for this project was invaluable. I must also thank all five of Mr. Clement's children—Sarah, Ellen, Anne, Doug, and David, for their support. Anne and Doug offered much-appreciated encouragement while Ellen provided some of the early materials and leads necessary to get this project off of the ground. Sarah and David in particular were my partners in developing the book's manuscript, offering valued advice and support along the way. Mr. Clement's two step-children, Michael and Cindy, were also crucial supporters and helped to keep me motivated and on-track.

I am indebted to one of my star students (now a Christopher Newport University alumna), Lizzy Wall, for the critical role that she played in transcribing large sections of Mr. Clement's original writing. Lizzy's able assistance sped up the completion time for this book by several months at the very least. The faculty and staff at the United States Military Academy at West Point were also very supportive of this project and they have my eternal thanks. Finally, I am most grateful to my own family—particularly my wife Katey and our two children, S.J. and Emma—for their patience and inspiration as I saw this project through. As someone who knew and learned from Mr. Clement as a young man, it was an honor to help put his fascinating World War II reflections into print. I hope that they can inform, inspire, and instruct future generations of historians, military personnel, and leadership practitioners in the same manner that they have helped me.

Sean M. Heuvel, Ph.D.
Department of Leadership and American Studies
Christopher Newport University, Newport News, Virginia
July 2016

Chapter 1

Early Years in Cambridge

I was born at Cambridge City Hospital, Cambridge, Massachusetts, on July 22, 1918. It was also my mother's birthday (Helen Theresa Murphy), who was 28 years old at the time. Dad (Arthur J. Clement) was an immigrant. His family came from Montreal, Canada about 1895. He was a "derivative citizen," naturalized when his father, Charles Clement, was naturalized. Dad was 31 years old when I was born. I was the second of three boys—between Arthur J. Clement (born in 1916) and Lawrence Clement (born in 1921).

I was educated at a series of parochial schools operated by the Sisters of St. Joseph.[1] I entered the first grade at age five at St. Paul's School[2] on Mt. Auburn Street in Cambridge. I still remember my first day, sitting in the back of the room, having been deposited by my mother; and bolting out of the door in tears headed for home. The second grade was a traumatic experience. I attended a boarding school, St. Domenic's Academy, because mother had heart problems and was in the hospital frequently. Dad visited on weekends, and it was terrible when he left, I crying and clinging to him, and a nun grabbing my free arm and assuring him that I would be alright. How hard it must have been on him—it certainly was on me. I was at St. Paul's through the fifth grade, living at 9 Banks Street off of Mt. Auburn. We moved to Arlington (Hardwick Street) when I was 10, and I attended Saint Agnes School.[3] Here, Mother insisted that I take piano lessons, although I preferred baseball and hockey. Lessons were given by a nun, who also

---

[1]   The Sisters of St. Joseph is a Roman Catholic religious congregation of women that was founded in Le Puy-en-Velay, France in 1650. It has had a presence in the United States since the 19th century.

[2]   Today, there is a St. Paul's Choir School—founded in 1963—that operates in that general location.

[3]   Founded in 1888, Saint Agnes School continues to operate today in Arlington, Massachusetts as a Catholic prep school for grades Pre-K through 8th.

administered rapped knuckles discipline when it was obvious that I hadn't practiced. Many years later I found out that Mother had been a very fine piano player; we never had a piano and I never heard her play. How sad it seems to me now. Her love for the piano resulted in my wasted lessons. My seventh grade year was at a new school in Brighton, a Boston suburb, called Our Lady of the Presentation School.[4] We lived on Hunnewell Avenue. I graduated from grammar school here in 1931.

Early on it was discovered that I had a good singing voice—good enough for the Catholic choir. I was recruited in the first grade and was issued a cassock and surplice. I was soon singing at the high mass at St. Paul's[5] in Latin. I have not forgotten snatches of the service: *Dominus vobiscum* (I can play dominoes better than you can, according to Dad), *orate fratres, pater noster, et cum spiritu tuo,* etc. Dad was not a regular churchgoer until I made the choir; Mom went regularly. They both attended the lengthy high mass to see their little boy perform—talk about support.

Christmases were special of course. The custom then was to put the tree up on Christmas Eve, to the delight and surprise of the children early Christmas morning. Aunt Jenny (Dad's sister) was a customary Christmas visitor and we all looked forward to her coming. She brought an enthusiasm and cheery spirit to the occasion, arriving in time to help decorate and staying for a few days. Carrol, her husband, a dour Yankee, would arrive on Christmas day; he worked for United Shoe[6] in the little country town of Beverly.[7] We loved to visit Aunt Jen out there in the country. Favorite gifts included books and sporting goods—baseball gloves, shoes, bats, balls, hockey skates,

---

[4] Located in Brighton, Massachusetts, Our Lady of the Presentation School closed in 2005 as part of broader cost-saving measures by the local Catholic Diocese. Following intense lobbying by the local community, it re-opened in 2012 as a community center.

[5] The Parish of Saint Paul Roman Catholic Church in Harvard Square has been in continuous operation since at least 1875.

[6] The United Shoe Machinery Corporation first formed in 1899 and opened a large, ten-acre factory in Beverly a few years later. The factory remained in operation until the 1980s. Since then, the Cummings Center has restored and enlarged the impressive structure and once more provided a place of employment for hundreds of workers.

[7] Beverly is a small city in Essex County, Massachusetts, located along the state's North Shore.

sticks, footballs, and pads. Gifts would be hidden to be found under the tree on Christmas morning—early.

The turbulent depression years and Dad's loss of income resulted in all of those moves I described above. Dad was a self-made man. I don't believe he finished high school in East Cambridge. However, his employ at Leavitt & Peirce's tobacco shop, Harvard Square, brought contact with students and faculty.[8] He was in his twenties and quick to appreciate the value of an education, as was Mother. It was understood early on that we would go to college, Harvard of course, as day students. This plan seemed feasible enough before the 1929 crash. The depression brought change, reflected in our many moves. Let me explain.

Dad learned the tobacco business at the famous Leavitt & Peirce shop. Tobacco and billiards have been associated with Leavitt's since it was founded in 1883. Dad played a very good game of billiards, and in fact won a bit of money from unsuspecting students. It was thought that he would manage Leavitt's in time; in fact I am named for Wallace Peirce, an owner. Around 1915, Dad with some backers opened up his own shop in the basement of the Lampoon Building on Mt. Auburn Street, just off the Square.[9] Dad had just married Mother; he was 28. It was Arthur's Restaurant and Smoke Shop, Inc. and it was successful. He did mail order business when the College let out for the summer. The *Harvard Lampoon* is a well-known humor magazine, matched by Yale's *Boola Boola*.[10] The building is a triangular shaped two story affair, mocking a medieval castle in design. The baronial hall upstairs had maces and armor and a huge banquet table. Meals could be brought up via a dumb waiter out of Dad's kitchen. The Harvard-Yale game weekend brought the biennial banquet for the *Lampoon* and *Boola Boola* staffs—many pranks and perhaps a few drinks and good cheer. One remarkable story involved the janitor, Bob Stewart (alias Bob Lampoon), a diminutive Scot with a brogue. He was a favorite of the *Lampoon* staff—colorful, funny, and often in his cups. One Yale game weekend Bob got drunk and was served stripped and passed out on the dumb waiter to the cheers of the celebrants.

---

[8] Established in 1883, Leavitt & Peirce continues to operate today in Harvard Square.

[9] The Harvard Lampoon Building was built in 1909 using a mock Flemish architectural design. It is best known as the home of the *Harvard Lampoon*, a popular undergraduate humor publication at Harvard.

[10] "Boola Boola" is also a fight song of Yale University.

The first home I remember was at 69 ½ Mt. Auburn Street, across from the Lampoon. It was a single family, two-story, white frame building, long since replaced by a block of College buildings. It had a fenced in yard. Barbed wire was attached to the top to deter Lawrence, typically, from escaping. This was to no avail on one occasion when he disappeared. He was found in Harvard Square, standing on top of the subway entrance dancing for the benefit of the passersby. Nappy Williams, a noted black cab driver and a good friend of Dad's, had my brother in tow. Nappy was the cab driver for the exclusive Porcellian Club [11] and its wealthy student clientele. Dad would charter Nappy to drive us to baseball games at Fenway Park and Braves Field—real style. And there is a story of Nappy driving a fare to the airport one night, having a drink or two, and getting out on the landing strip. The green lights meant go and he did, right into the bay. He survived. We had a spare bedroom at 69 ½ and let it out to students. The latter included Oliver La Farge, [12] noted sociologist and author of one of my favorite books, *Laughing Boy*; Tom Braden, a Harvard place-kicker on a rare scholarship; and Fritz and later Charlie Delafield [13] of a New York banking family. Referencing Charlie, I remember being irked at Dad because he felt Charlie had complimented him by saying, "Arthur, you may be a shopkeeper but you are a gentleman." I felt even then that my blood was not "ditchwater"—Napoleon's expression. [14]

---

[11] Founded in the early 1790s, the Porcellian Club is a men-only final club at Harvard University, similar to Yale's Skull and Crossbones or Princeton's Ivy Club. A local urban legend maintains that if members of the Porcellian do not earn their first million before they turn 40, the Club will give it to them.

[12] A direct descendant of Commodore Oliver Hazard Perry (1785-1819), Oliver La Farge (1901-1963) earned his BA from Harvard in 1924 along with an MA in 1929.

[13] Charles Delafield (1905-1998) graduated from Harvard in 1927 and went on to become an executive with Consolidated Edison in New York. Following his retirement from Con Edison in 1969, he was appointed by Gov. Nelson Rockefeller to serve on a state horse racing commission. His ancestor John Delafield, who arrived in America in 1783, brought to America the first copy of the treaty of peace which formally concluded the American Revolution.

[14] In a furious response to an aborted assassination attempt, Napoleon's exact quote was, "Is my blood ditchwater? Am I a dog to be shot down in the street? I will soon teach these Bourbons a lesson they will not soon forget."

I have always been interested in sports, both as a participant and as an observer. These interests included baseball, football, hockey, swimming in my early days; later, boxing, tennis, some golf, and to an extent shooting and fishing, thanks to my former brother-in-law, Pep Mansfield, an expert Kentuckian sportsman. I always had an interest in horses and was delighted with the riding instruction at the Point and with my later cavalry service. I'm sure my father had an influence on my interests. Dad had been a very fine baseball player: pitcher and infielder, a good batter, fast, with a strong arm. He said that he could have had a scholarship to Dean Academy [15] but had to work to support the family. Early memories include Dad taking Arthur and me to Fenway Park to see the Yankees play the Sox—Babe Ruth, Lou Gehrig et al. I was about nine or ten. I also remember an incident when we all jumped up to see a play and the fellow behind hit Arthur with a newspaper to have him sit down. Dad whirled around, cursed the fellow, and started to punch him. We, very embarrassed, tugged on Dad, the fellow apologized, and Dad sat down. No one was going to touch one of his boys.

Baseball has always been my favorite sport. As a boy in grammar school I remember the pick-up teams we had and the various parks, playgrounds, and back lots we used. We played with two, three, or more players using tennis balls if need be. I remember Lawrence and I playing in our back yard in Allston using the house as a backstop and the garage as the outfield wall. Certain sections of the garage were marked off for singles, doubles, triples, and home runs; over the garage was an out. We had five swings each, using part of a broomstick as a bat; used a tennis ball; and batted left-handed. Each turn at bat was half an inning. Another game played with three was running bases. Here two players were at a base a nominal distance apart. The idea was for the third player to run from one base to the other without being tagged out. This involved speed, sliding ability, and the ability to fake running in one direction and then breaking in the other.

We organized our teams for all sports. One neighborhood in general supported one team. Little league was non-existent. Boston was the home of the American League Red Sox and National League Braves. Early on we became knowledgeable fans. Our heroes were usually from the visiting teams, since the Boston teams were not doing too well. Dad taught me to keep score, something I still do when at a

---

[15] Established in 1865, Dean College is a private college located in Franklin, Massachusetts. It was originally named Dean Academy.

game. And what players we saw: Ruth, Gehrig, Lazzeri, Crossetti, Dickey, the Waner brothers, Pie Traynor, Arky Vaughan, Al Simmons, Jimmie Foxx, Joe Cronin, Heinie Manush, Lefty Grove, the Dean brothers, Earl Averill, Charlie Gehringer, Gabby Hartnett, Carl Hubbell, Hal Shumacher, Bill Terry, and on and on. The radio announcer for those games was Fred Hoey.[16] They could learn from him today. He stayed with the game—balls, strikes, play-by-play. He didn't bore the listener with unrelated trivia or attempts at locker room humor. In other words, he respected the game and was all business. So many TV persons seem to get bored with the game these days and feel they have to keep talking to earn their keep. Proctor and Lowenstein of Home Team Sports are among the worst. Hoey was a pro. I can still hear his "Here's the windup, here's the pitch, and there's a smash into left center good for a base hit." God bless you Fred wherever you are; you liked baseball.

Another real champion was Bob Coyne, the sports cartoonist for the *Boston Post*, a morning paper.[17] He captured the highlights with a few beautifully simple cartoons, complete with pithy dialogue. I can still see his Babe; big number three on his back, legs twisted, swing finished with a semicircle portraying the arc, a big burst at the point of impact, and accompanying words "good bye!" An error on a ground ball portrayed by a bow-legged infielder, hands cupped near his knees, the ball shown bouncing through his legs and into the outfield with the caption "oops!" Another showing Gehrig tripling to right, churning around the bases with the third baseman yelling to the outfielder, "Turn it, Dusty (Dusty Cooke, right fielder)!" We often sneaked into the parks, Fenway being much more difficult than Braves field. When the cop had turned the corner on his beat we'd climb the fence and get lost with fans in the bleachers. Another way was to get to the park early and line up to turn the ticket stiles. The ticket taker would let in about four at each stile, turned as each fan entered. The first three boys got in during practice, the fourth during the first inning.

Some of those neighborhood boys were good ball players with fascinating names: Idoo Fallon, a natural ball player, one of the best; Neil Keleher, a big left-handed first baseman, quiet and steady (with a very pretty sister); Joe Artesani; Fatty Bagley, anything but fat, a natural

---

[16] Fred Hoey (1885-1949) called games for the Boston Braves from 1925 to 1938 and for the Boston Red Sox from 1927 to 1938.

[17] Harold Victor "Bob" Coyne (1898-1976) drew sports cartoons for several Boston newspapers for over 40 years.

athlete and superb hockey player; Mundo Dimateo, all-around athlete and a vicious tackler with instinctive timing for the hit; Paul LeBlanc, a triple threat quarterback who fired a bullet pass; Johnny Hill, our catcher and the only black I remember playing with, a long ball hitter with a strong arm, always laughing and having fun; Red Gilooley, shortstop and fiery competitor; Eddie Gincauskas, a big, Polish fast ball pitcher (also called Eddie Bananas). And some of the neighborhood gangs had colorful names: "The Barn Rats," from a locale near the trotting horse stables near the Charles River in Allston; "the Blocks AC," from a nearby tenement district; "the Polocks," a tough bunch of good athletes from a Polish enclave.

Memorable baseball moments from those days include a Fourth of July, about 1931, when I managed our team and played second base. Smith Playground, Allston, had arranged for our team to play the Polocks for a $10 prize. I selected our ten best, and we won three to two, a dollar apiece, a fortune then. The next year we played again and lost. I had a chance to be a hero but fanned with the bases loaded. I ran home in tears, slammed my glove across the room and vowed never to play the game again. Mom and Dad commiserated and I was out there again in a couple of days. I made the team as a senior in high school. I had a great game against Lawrence Academy, going five for five. This was quite unusual since I was generally "good field, no hit." I made my letter and was proud of that. I played football for our neighborhood team, very light but fast and elusive. I could kick and pass pretty well. Many an hour was spent in pickup games with my brothers and playmates.

Football season meant Harvard football games. Dad had influence and was able to get us jobs selling programs at the stadium. We got a penny a program but more importantly saw the game. I guess my first impression of West Point was when the Army team came to town and the cadets paraded into the stadium. Cambridge and Boston loved the cadets and turned out en masse to see them, unlike those blasé New Yorkers as I found out later. Barry Wood was the great Harvard athlete of the era (early 1930's), All American, Phi Beta Kappa, baseball captain, hockey and tennis standout.[18] He was matched by little Albie

---

[18] William Barry Wood Jr. (1910-1971) was elected to the College Football Hall of Fame in 1980. Following his athletic career and 1932 Harvard graduation, he went on to an academic career in medicine and microbiology, teaching at Washington University at St. Louis and Johns Hopkins University.

Booth of Yale.[19] I remember the thrill of being introduced to Barry Wood in Dad's restaurant. As a businessman in the Square, Dad had many connections with the College. We were able to use the gym facilities and the pool. We also saw many hockey games at the Boston Garden. The Widener Library was a favorite spot, in the Harvard Yard.

Summer vacations were a memorable part of those early days. Dad closed his business, accommodating to the College schedule. He had a good mail order tobacco business, however, which kept him in town during the week while we vacationed. Francestown (in New Hampshire), Ipswich, Marshfield, and Duxbury afforded rental properties for us. We rented a farmhouse in the little village of Francestown for a couple of summers. The owner, an elderly gentleman who we called "Granpa Foote," stayed there. He was a widower whose wife had hung herself on the stairway leading upstairs; very spooky and we never went upstairs. His horse was named "Pet," who got our undivided attention; watering, feeding, grooming, stall cleaning, and bareback riding around the barnyard. Granpa Foote would hitch Pet up to his carriage for local shopping trips and we loved it. When I read a Robert Frost poem now, I invariably think of that little village and the old farm.

Ipswich, famous for its fried clams, provided a beach house and the beach. The Ipswich River ran close by. One day we and some other boys found a small rowboat down by the river. We improvised paddles and followed the tide out. We played around on a sandbar, not noticing the tide turning very swiftly. Finally aware we started to paddle back upstream. Arthur (a.k.a. "Junior"—he always went by that), the oldest, took charge giving us orders to paddle. We all pitched in with one exception—Lawrence. He refused to take orders and wouldn't paddle unless Junior did. Meanwhile, Dad appeared on the river bank, shouting at us to land, worried about what might happen. He was a pretty good swimmer and we probably could have handled being capsized, except for Lawrence and those tricky currents. Anyway, we made it to shore and got a couple of spanks to deter future voyages.

Marshfield was the site of the Cape Cod Camp and Country Club—CCC&CC.[20] It had well-to-do Jewish patrons, summer cabins

---

[19] Known as "Little Boy Blue" for his small stature, Albie Booth (1908-1959) went on to a career in coaching following his athletic achievements at Yale. He was elected to the College Football Hall of Fame in 1966.

[20] This may be the modern Marshfield Country Club, which was founded in 1922.

and cottages, a recreation center, dining hall, stables, and an active social program. Dad had the concession for meals and a concession stand, employing his kitchen staff. Arthur and I were sometimes in charge of the stand during slack periods. I thought it was silly to sell a cigar for 12 cents, with tax, so I rounded off to a dime. We also would refill half empty soft drinks and resell them, not wanting to waste anything. Of course Dad never knew. Boat excursions with picnic lunches were fun, we being included with the group. Nightly entertainments were held, slightly risqué as I recall, but we managed to sneak a peek. Twenty-five cents an hour for horseback rides and I had a few. The chef's wife, a nice young lady, would volunteer to take me along now and then, a nice treat.

The Maryknoll Order had a retreat in the vicinity, and we attended church there.[21] I was in the eighth grade and ready for high school in a year. Boarding school was out of the question unless I decided to become a priest and was admitted to Maryknoll. So I talked to Mother into getting an interview with an admissions cleric. "Come back in a year" was the outcome. That was the end of my calling. We had great times at some of those beaches. Humarock near Ipswich, noted for its pounding breakers after the storm. We loved to dive under those huge waves catching them just before they broke. Crane's Beach, also near Ipswich, a beautiful spot—now quite crowded I am told. Singing Beach in Manchester-by-the-Sea. Nantasket with its amusements. Plush times for the Clements.

And now back to the real world. The crash came in 1929 when Dad was 42 and I was 11, in the seventh grade. For a few years business had been off and we moved from Cambridge to Brighton. The Harvard House Plan insured that local restaurants would feel the pinch, since students were charged for meals in their houses (dorms). The well-off could afford to eat out of course. The result was that Dad declared bankruptcy. He did not "fall on his sword" as they say, but used his contacts to get a job in a clothing store on the Square. I look back on this now with admiration for my parents. They tried to keep the shock from us. Dad still joked and was optimistic about our future, although I certainly wasn't. Arthur was a day student at Harvard, a

---

[21] Maryknoll is a name shared by three organizations (two religious institutes and one lay ministry) that are part of the Roman Catholic Church: Maryknoll Fathers and Brothers (Catholic Foreign Mission Society of America; Maryknoll Society), Maryknoll Sisters (Maryknoll Sisters of St. Dominic), and Maryknoll Lay Missioners.

few hundred dollars tuition, an enormous amount to us. Mother insisted that we take day trips to the beach, by subway and trolley to South Boston and the L-Street Beach. Not like the good old days and those summers away. I was rather sad and sorry for Mom and the bold front she put on for our sake. The depression years had a lasting impact. I never had any great urge to own a business after Dad's experience. A well-ordered military career has suited me fine.

It was decided that I would go to Boston Latin School, the oldest public school in the country, founded in 1635—one year before Harvard.[22] Arthur was already attending, and Lawrence would later. I commuted by bus and trolley daily. A modest tuition was paid. The school was uncompromising in its approach to education, and still is I hear. The goal was to pass College Board exams, thereby qualifying for most colleges, Harvard included. Courses included four years of Latin, four of English, three of French, two of Greek, plus physics, math, and ancient and modern history. Much homework was given and 50% was passing, probably equal to 70% at most schools. I belong to the Alumni Association and apparently the standards remain high. Sports at Latin School included four years of track and baseball in my senior year. I was fast, competing in the 176-yard dash and medley relay. I played left field part-time, and you know about my five-for-five day.

I graduated in 1935 and was admitted to Harvard but couldn't attend because of the tuition. Arthur had a couple of years to go and it was decided that I would work for a year before entering. Something was bound to turn up, in the words of Dickens' Micawber.[23] I was disappointed and felt that my future meant a job like Dad's (aarg!). Anyway, Dad's connections got me work as an usher in the University Theater in the Square. I proudly gave Mom my $14 or $15 every Friday; I was contributing. I later got a better-paying job as office boy in the University Travel Bureau, also on the Square. I cleaned the place, ran errands, delivered tickets, and assisted in developing passport photos. Here I met Boris Leonardi, who handled overseas trips. He was of German extraction, well educated, and spoke with an accent. He had shipped out on a schooner in his youth and I had read Conrad's *Lord*

---

[22] Established on April 23, 1635, The Boston Latin School is considered both the first public school and oldest existing school in the United States. It has long been known as a bastion for educating Boston's prominent "Brahmin" elite.

[23] This is a reference to the fictional character "Wilkins Micawber" from Charles Dickens' 1850 novel, *David Copperfield*.

Jim. I was fascinated with some of Boris' stories. I wanted to go to sea. In fact, I applied at the Maritime Union office—unknown to my parents—on Atlantic Avenue, but was told to come back in a year when I was 18.

My chance for college came when I learned of appointments to Annapolis coming up. Congressman Richard M. Russell[24] was to hold competitive examinations for two appointments. First came the preliminary physical examination at the Boston Navy Yard. This was the first complete physical that I had ever taken. I did well except for the eye exam. My vision was fine but I was slightly red-green blind; I couldn't pick numbers out of those colored dots. I was really shaken and again wondered about my future. I was told by the examiners that the Army was not as demanding on color; colored yarns were used. I felt that it would be a waste of time but Dad and Mom felt otherwise. Two West Point competitive appointments were available. It all seemed so implausible; the idea of getting an appointment to either Academy. With faint heart I took the Army route. The Congressman's exam was on January 4, 1936, a date I will always remember. I took the Army preliminary physical at the Boston Army Base. Everything went well until the color test, first the dots which I failed but then the yarns which I passed. It was so simple. The sergeant picked out a yarn from a box and told me to match it with others. I did so easily, as well as several other colors. I never had to name them. So I am slightly color blind but good enough for the Army and for the Department of Motor Vehicles. And note that the idea of a military career appealed to me from the start.

I prepared thoroughly for the Congressional civil service examination. The subjects were to be history, mathematics, and English. I bought some pocket books of review material and planned my schedule. Aunt Kittie (Mother's sister) and Uncle Herb had a nice home in Milton, and no children—peace and quiet. They had me stay with them for a week or 10 days while I studied. I had worked out a schedule, so many days for each subject and a review. I stayed on schedule and then used the West Point examination pamphlet for general review. When January 4 came I was ready. Boston Latin School was my savior. Examinations were at the Boston Army Base and took about

---

[24] U.S. Rep. Richard M. Russell (1891-1977) represented the 9th Congressional District of Massachusetts between 1935 and 1937 and was also a mayor of Cambridge. He was the son of Massachusetts Gov. William Russell (1857-1896), who served in that office between 1891 and 1894.

six hours. About 50 or 60 were competing for two principal appointments. I was exhausted at the finish but felt that I had done well. It was such a long shot and it was difficult to picture myself as a cadet, pursuing an Army career. We lived at 31 Bayard Street, Allston, in the shadow of Harvard Stadium. Dad's French Canadian mother, Grammie, was staying with us at the time, a wonderful old lady. Her prayers probably had something to do with the outcome.

We called her "Grammie," her name being Clotilde LeFrancois. She was born in the 1860s and I remember her saying that she had two brothers who fought in the Civil War, one for the North and one for the South—mercenaries.[25] She remembered that one died in a prison camp in the South. Her home town was a village called La Prairie, outside of Montreal. We loved to hear her tell of when the Indians used to come for food, and she would hide. She married Charles Clement, probably about 1880. I say this because Father was born in 1887, and he had several older siblings. She had 13 children in all, but five survived; Clotilda (Aunt Tillie), Alphonse (Uncle Al), Aunt Rose, Dad (Arthur—pronounced "Archure" by Grammie), and Genevieve (Aunt Jennie). My Grandfather died shortly after the move down from Canada to Cambridge, Massachusetts, leaving Grammie to cope. And cope she did—a remarkable woman.

I know nothing about how she actually managed to settle in, survive, and raise a family. She operated a small store in East Cambridge and brought up the family there. Grammie was a very staunch Catholic, and also a great admirer of Queen Victoria, wearing her hair in tight braids, wrapped up like the Queen's. She lived with us for short periods as I grew up—neat dignified, immaculate, and always cheerful. She had a delightful French accent and some fascinating versions of various English words. For example, ice chest was "hyster"; to light the stove was to "lit the gas"; my name was "Warnie"; Arthur became "Archure"; if we teased we were told to "go lang with you or I'll give you a clack"; and a term of endearment was *cher petit rat*—"dear little rat." She took our teasing in good spirits and would laugh with us at her mistakes.

My Mother—of South Boston Irish Catholic upbringing—I know loved her Canadian mother-in-law as we loved her. A priest came weekly to hear her confession and administer communion since

---

[25] Subsequent research has thus far been unable to determine neither the names of these individuals nor the specific nature of their Civil War service.

Grammie couldn't make it to church because of arthritis. Her room was always immaculate; in one corner was a statue of the Sacred Heart, with a votive candle generally lit before it. She said her rosary regularly. I still remember her rocking my younger brother to sleep, crooning softly in a low monotone, enough to hypnotize anyone. She never learned to speak English very well, but Dad talked to her in French. He never spoke French to us. I guess he was proud that he had no trace of an accent, just like the boys he grew up with. My Grandmother was loved by Murphys and Clements alike. A strong woman, good, kind, and loving. I'm sure she has a favored spot above now.

Anyway, a few weeks later when I came home from work Grammie met me at the door saying in her broken English; "Warnie, Warnie I sing (sign) for telegram." Then she gave it to me. It announced that I had been appointed and would take the entrance exam on March 4 at the now familiar Army Base. I was stunned, and deliriously happy. I grabbed Gram and danced around the room shouting that she had brought me luck and that it wouldn't have happened without her. She was excited and laughing, too. We were all proud of what I had done, and you can be sure that the family was quickly informed. The March 4 exam was anticlimactic, but also quite difficult. I thought that I had passed but wasn't really sure. I finally got word and was instructed to report to West Point on July 1, 1936 with only essential belongings. I was on my way!

Chapter 2

West Point and the Cavalry

JUNE 30, 1936 found me on a Boston-New York overnight Pullman en route to the Academy—my first train ride. The porter got me off on time in the morning (I found out later that he had been tipped by my Dad). A cab took me to the Weehawken Ferry and the Hudson River. The West Shore Line train took me up the river to my destination. I had some company along the way, future classmates, and we talked quietly about what might be in store. The road from the station goes uphill to the barracks area, an endless march it seemed. We were directed to a nearby sally port[26] for our welcoming. A cadet at a desk checked me in, told me that I was in G Company, and directed me through the sally port into the quadrangular barracks area. My life changed dramatically right then.

I was now a plebe, plebian, freshman. "Drop that bag mister! Roll up those trouser legs! Pull those shoulders back! Front those slimy green eyes Mr. Ducrot."[27] I made the mistake of grinning at the last command; it sounded so much like what I had read about the place. I was immediately corrected by about three of my captors, second year men, recent plebes, especially selected for the beast detail. I was now in the recruit phase of training called beast barracks. We immediately began close order drill, marching in step, eyes to the front, shoulders down and back, double timing now and then, and being constantly corrected. The barber shop was a welcome respite followed by the tailor shop, and then the issuance of equipment. The latter was carried double time across the quadrangle up three flights of stairs to an as-

---

[26] A sally port is a secure, controlled entryway to a fortification or prison.

[27] At West Point during this era, new cadets who made mistakes received quick correction from a stern, non-commissioned officer cadet, who often addressed the infractor as "Mr. Ducrot."

signed room, shared by Walter Winton[28] and Ray Downey.[29] By the end of the day we were marching in formation in uniform: gray dress cap, shirt and trousers. We also found out then that women wear pants and men wear trousers. Culture shock had set in and we were numb. Every minute had been supervised. We even took our first shower in the basement together. The bugle sounding *Taps* for the first time for us was a welcome end to the day. I had no time to even think of being home sick.

Let me digress to explain cadet nomenclature for the four classes. First year men were plebes, plebeians, constituting the fourth class. Yearlings were second year men, the third class. Cows were third year men. First classmen were just that, although they might be referred to as "firsties," but not in their presence. The next six weeks brought an intensive training schedule. Military drill and weapons instruction, gymnastics, boxing, wrestling, fencing, ball room dancing and etiquette. In a couple of weeks we underwent a practice demerit system. Demerits were given for infractions of the rules. Over 20 demerits in a month meant punishment tours, marching on free time—Wednesday and Saturday. Early on we had sessions on the honor system. You would be expelled for lying, cheating, stealing or failing to report an honor infraction. An infraction of regulations brought demerits but an honor infraction meant dismissal. We also began intensive singing sessions—Army football songs and other traditional pieces, including the words to the bugle calls. We were issued a booklet, *The Plebe Bible*, and were required to memorize it, and recite on call.

Spectators at West Point parades have no idea of the constant murmur in ranks just out of earshot. Plebes are in the front rank, upperclassmen in the rear. Plebes are being constantly quizzed and braced

---

[28] Tennessee native Walter Ferrell Winton, Jr. (1917-2007) graduated from West Point in 1940 and went on to perform distinguished service during World War II, seeing action in such famous battles as the Normandy invasion, Operation Market Garden, and the Battle of the Bulge. Following service in the Korean War, he reached the rank of brigadier general and retired from the U.S. Army in 1970.

[29] Massachusetts native Raymond J. Downey (1915-1981) also graduated from West Point in 1940 and served in the U.S. Army Air Corps during World War II. His bomber was shot down over Italy in November 1943, but he managed to evade capture and made it back to Allied lines after the liberation of Rome in 1944. Downey went on to serve in the U.S. Air Force and retired in 1961 at the rank of colonel.

NOTHING IMPOSSIBLE

(posture correction). "Let's see some wrinkles in those shoulders, mister. Squeeze them back. What are the pieces for parade, mister?" There were three pieces to be memorized daily, along with the authors; the march on, the pass in review, and the march off. If you didn't know the music and your interrogator did, then you would appear at his room at reveille, fully dressed, and brace against the wall.

There was a certain protocol when a cadet passed out at parade, usually a plebe on a hot summer day. When he slumped to the ground a detail of two rear rank cadets—first classmen—came forward, loosened his gear and got him to the rear. Meanwhile the formation was restored preparatory to the pass in review. It was the first classmen who got out of the parade, not necessarily the closest to the victim. Another custom was to have plebes sing the *Missouri National* while the rest were dressing for parade. "Every time I pray for rain the darned old sun comes out again. The sun shines bright while I get dressed but it rains like hell at parade rest." This seldom brought rain and subsequent parade cancellation. A cadet who had passed out was not necessarily off the hook. He was queried as to what he had eaten before the formation. If he had indulged at the boodle shop (ice cream parlor) he got two demerits for improper diet; note how the honor system required a truthful answer.

Anyways, time passed and we began to focus on academics. We took a basic engineering course in order to eventually earn our BS degrees. Foreign languages included two years of French and one of Spanish—I guess that covered our borders with Canada and Mexico. A favorite was military history—taken in our first class year; Napoleon, Civil War, World War I. Texts included Jomini's multi-volume biography of Napoleon,[30] Henderson's *Stonewall Jackson*,[31] and Steele's

---

[30] This is likely *Vie politique et militaire de Napoléon* (first published in 1827), by Baron Jomini Antoine-Henri (1779-1869), a Swiss officer who served in both the French and Russian armies. He was one of the most celebrated writers on the Napoleonic Art of war, and his books were long utilized at many military academies.

[31] This was British Army officer G.F.R. Henderson's (1854-1903) work, *Stonewall Jackson and the American Civil War* (first published in 1898). Henderson served during the Second Boer War and later became a colonel in the British Army.

Campaigns.[32] Equitation instruction was given for the four years.[33] Boxing was an intercollegiate sport then, and we always fielded a good team. Leaves were taken each Christmas beginning with yearling year; one summer vacation was taken second class summer. First classmen were allowed six weekends.

Overall, I adapted to the Army lifestyle, although not painlessly. I was no stranger to the area and in fact was a first class buck. An average student, I was a better than average athlete. I played baseball for four years and also won the intercollegiate boxing championship in 1940. I enjoyed my cadet days and knew from the start that I wanted an Army career. My roommate accurately described me in the *Howitzer*:

> The whole of a quantity is, in personalities as in mathematics, equal to the sum of all its parts. Outcroppings of Clem's character included the glee with which he precipitated hallway riots by some outrageous word or act and his preoccupation with bad fiction and good military history. Included too were his graceful finished competence on the hockey rink, in the boxing ring, and on the baseball diamond. Moreover, he managed to combine unfailing consideration with high-spirited swagger.

On graduation I ranked high enough to be commissioned in the horse cavalry, June 11, 1940. Enrollment was 1800 when I graduated. My class had 449 members, a 25% attrition rate from beginning strength.

And so we graduated, leaving regimentation and strict disciplinary stands of the Point, and entering the real world of peacetime—the Regular Army with its very strong NCO corps. The Army was not much changed from 1918. Strength about 200,000: three infantry divisions at about 2/3 strength, six with understrength brigades; two cavalry divisions under peacetime strength, with a few understrength separate regiments. There was a Coast Artillery Corps, with its beautiful posts on each coast. No Anti-Aircraft Artillery branch. No Armor branch. West Point truly represented the combined arms team. The Air Corps

---

[32] This was Matthew Forney Steele's (1861-1953) *American Campaigns* (first published in 1909). Steele had served as a U.S. Army colonel and taught at the U.S. Army Command and Staff College from 1903 to 1909.

[33] Equitation is the art and practice of horsemanship and horse riding.

was part of the Army, with 12 B-17s and no tactical fighters. The Navy was our front line of defense and it had budget priority for modernization. At this time, Germany had 90 divisions and blitzkrieg; Japan had 50 divisions in China. Money was scarce: 1% GNP was spent on defense, versus over 5% now; and 1% of the defense budget was spent on R&D, versus 8% now. The Army had World War I stocks, a few light tanks, no tactical air, and a few bombers whose mission was coastal defense. "Never since Jefferson's time had America... been in so pacifist a mood as in 1933-1939; Hitler was canny enough to play on this," quoting Samuel Eliot Morison in his *History of the American People*. And Roosevelt's third term campaign emphasized "no foreign wars." Our service schools kept the faith, knowing if anything did happen we would be the trained cadre.

Anyway, in June 1940 I was assigned with the troopers of the 11th Cavalry on the Mexican border in Southern California. This experience made an indelible impression on me as I never forgot those formative years under the tutelage of the "Old Army" noncoms, a vanishing breed. What also made a powerful impression on me were the incredible horses with which I worked. I have always liked horses although born and bred a city boy. I'm sure that had something to do with choosing the cavalry as my branch on graduation from West Point in 1940. At any rate, before joining the 11th Cavalry my first assignment was to the Cavalry School, Fort Riley, Kansas in August 1940. About 30 or 40 of my classmates were also assigned there with a contingent of others recently commissioned in the Regular Army from the Reserve Corps, and a fine group they were. We were all to take the First Basic Horse and Mechanized Course. The mechanized part was a tip of the hat to the arrival of armor on the battlefields of Europe and the German blitzkrieg. You must remember that we were still an infantry-oriented Army, a heritage of World War I experience. Only the Germans and Russians had adopted the new armor doctrine with an emphasis on firepower and movement. But I digress.

Horses I recall at Fort Riley included Reno Kent, Swing Hi, and Nebraska. The first was a thoroughbred, one of several Reno horses, and a good mount. However, he disliked ditch jumps, and needed urging on brush jumps. I learned of his failings the hard way, being thrown into a ditch and into brush jumps on a couple of occasions. As I recall, I never lost the reins, and thus managed to hold onto the horse each time, a slight consolation. Nebraska was not my mount but was unforgettable in that he broke wind each time he jumped. He could be heard throughout the column. But he was a real competitor and a willing jumper. Swing Hi was a small horse about 152, with a big heart. He was a noted jumper with a beautiful disposition. He took any and all jumps and loved to compete. Although I was not a gifted horseman by any means, Swing Hi made me look very good. I was quite proud when I came in third in our class competition aboard this horse.

I believe I had only one bad spill with Swing Hi, but it was not his fault. Our platoon was taking a cross country ride including jumps of all sort—downhill, uphill, brush, timber, and ditch. On one particular stretch we were galloping along a ridge line which had some telegraph poles strung on our left flank. I was on the left toward the rear, with dust obscuring vision to the front. Suddenly, a telegraph pole loomed into view straight ahead. I tried to bring Swing Hi to the left but he had committed to the right. The pole caught my upraised arm and took me over the horse's croup in a complete somersault. I landed in the dust unharmed but rather embarrassed. Captain Raguse, our instructor (former Olympic Team), rode back to me with my horse. He asked me if I were alright and told me to remount, obviously rather disgusted with my performance. I could tell by his expression and the way he said: "Mount Mr. Clement and let's continue the ride."

Now that I have mentioned Captain Carl Raguse I must tell you a little about him. He was probably the finest horseman in the Army at that time and had competed in the Olympics. He was always well turned out, rather slim, tall, and with a slight moustache. The latter was promptly affected by one or two of my classmates. I never heard Captain Raguse raise his voice, or saw him lose patience with us or with the animals. That quiet command to "get your heels down" or the observation that he could "see daylight" were enough to make us take immediate corrective action. On occasion he would take an especially unruly horse and within minutes have the animal performing like a champion. Wherever you are, Captain Raguse, I salute you. A real role model as they say today. Further research shows that Carl W.A. Raguse graduated from West Point along with 404 others in 1924; he ranked 102 in his class. He was on the Olympic Riding Team in 1932 and 1936.[34]

---

[34] Carl W. "Rags" Raguse (1902-1988) served in several administrative capacities during World War II—focusing mostly in purchasing and breeding management for U.S. Army horses—and retired from the Army as a full colonel in 1954. He later served as registered judge for the American Horse Show Association in dressage, hunters, jumpers, hunt seat equitation.

I left Fort Riley at the completion of the course in November and drove on to the West Coast to report to my regiment, the 11th Cavalry, stationed at the Presidio of Monterey, California. I might add that my first official duty was to supervise loading the troop box car—Troop E—preparatory to the regiment's move down to the Mexican border. Loading box cars had never been included in any course curriculum up to that time, but I found that there were and are many firsts experienced as you travel life's highway. You must learn to adapt quickly. Anyway, I was introduced to my first horse in E Troop a few days after joining. I was the Machine Gun Platoon leader, and very proud of my first command. Sergeant Wayne was my platoon sergeant. And New Deal was the horse selected for me, by Wayne I suppose. We were scheduled for a couple of hours of horse exercise, a great time filler in the cavalry. Generally the troopers rode one horse and led another in this outing.

You can imagine the feelings of a new lieutenant joining his platoon for the first time, under the critical eyes of all with more experience than the leader. In fact Wayne had about 20 years' service then, and the recruits had at least one or two years. I am now reminded of my very good friend Duane Cason, who was troop clerk at the time, a corporal. He was commissioned during the war and we served together at the Armored School and were later with the Research Analysis Corporation, both of us retired and he a colonel. He and Dottie later had a lovely place at Hilton Head Island.[35] Anyway, Wayne saluted and introduced himself and had my orderly—yes, I had one, PFC Martinez—lead up New Deal. He was a little skittish as I mounted but I had rather expected something of the sort. I got on, shortened the reins and held his head up to prevent bucking, and gave the arm signal to move out. We rode in column of two's with Wayne slightly to my left rear. Normally he would ride in rear of the platoon but he acted as guide and advisor on this day. New Deal quickly established himself as a jigger. He walked in a very jerky manner, bouncing up and down continually. This headache-insuring gait was relieved only at the trot, which we alternated with the walk. I said nothing to Wayne, but resolved to get a better mount when I could.

The regiment moved south to the Mexican border in November, shortly after I joined. My squadron, the 2nd, was located near a cross-

---

[35]   The late Col. Duane Cason served in both World War II and Vietnam. He retired from the U.S. Army in 1969.

roads called Campo, California,[36] about five miles from the Mexican border town of Tecate. We laid out a tent camp and a stable area with picket lines for the horses. Whereas my first home with the 11th had been a bungalow shared with another officer, my new home was a standard small-wall tent which I had to myself. Initially our duties consisted of familiarization trail rides, including correcting or expanding the rough maps which we had of the area. One of these rides led to my acquiring a new mount, albeit the hard way. New Deal was herd bound as were most of the animals, i.e. they did not like to be separated. Thus, when I volunteered to check a trail off the main path, while the troop continued on, New Deal was quite upset. After much prodding I got him headed down the trail, which gradually began to peter out. We were finally confronted with a huge boulder surrounded with mesquite and manzanita. I looked for a way around the obstacle paying little heed to my mount—a mistake. New Deal was alarmed at the situation and suddenly bucked straight up in the air. Caught by surprise, I was thrown over his head and made the gross mistake of losing the reins.

Now dismounted, I tried to coax the beast into allowing me to secure those dangling reins. He would have none of it and quickly whirled and started galloping, kicking and bucking through brush and rocks, headed in the general direction of the camp. Rather crestfallen and with serious doubts about my cavalry career, I followed his trail as best as I could. I found one stirrup along the way and later had to pay for its mate and for the saddle blanket. Luckily the saddle slid under his belly and he couldn't shake it, adding to his panic. As I walked back along the main trail, with a stirrup slung over my shoulder, I heard horses approaching. I knew that it was probably our ancient rivals, F Troop. They had been in camp when E Troop had left. I now was faced with a big decision: duck into the brush or continue the march. I decided to face the music and met the troop as it came up the trail. I saluted the troop commander and declined his offer of assistance. The column seemed endless as it went by, each platoon leader saluting in turn. They saved their ribald humor for later, back in camp. But I survived and I'm glad I decided to brazen it out—a very mortifying experience for a young lieutenant.

I finally got to camp and headed for the picket line. Sergeant Barnes, our aptly named stable sergeant, hurried over to ask how I was.

---

[36] Campo, California is located in the Mountain Empire area of southeastern San Diego County.

They were about to send out a search party. I'm sure Barnes was amused but he didn't show it. It seems that New Deal had arrived in style, at the gallop with saddle under belly and headed for the picket line where a few horses were tied. Barnes had grabbed a rake and hit the charging horse on the side of the head, opening up a cut but saving the line. New Deal was finally caught and led over to the veterinarian. Thus when I arrived I found the culprit tied up at the vet's, a huge bandage around his head but otherwise alright. I'm happy to say I never rode him again.

A shipment of remounts arrived at about this time. I was able to pick out one, a five-year-old, rather stocky, with black and white stockings and a star on his forehead, 15 ½ hands, named Ontario. They had all been processed at Fort Reno, Oklahoma, the remount station. Ontario had been halter broken but never ridden. He was sort of feisty but not mean. He was head shy and occasionally kicked. My orderly, PFC Martinez, and I worked with him daily for brief periods, getting him used to the bit and bridle. We assembled it piece by piece on his head all the while talking to him and feeding him bits of grain. Similarly, we finally slipped a saddle blanket on him, then the saddle, and finally the girth.

The day came when I decided to ride him. I led him out to the corral and had Martinez hold his head while I mounted. He immediately tried to cow kick with his left hind foot but I avoided it. I had a firm grip on the reins and kept his head up in approved style. Martinez retired to the shade of a tree to witness the proceedings. I gently applied leg pressure, but no spurs and he moved out. I circled the corral and was delighted with his movement. I decided to have him trot so applied pressure and touched him with the spurs. He responded by bucking and continued until he had discharged his cargo, namely me. I landed hard, spied Martinez convulsed with laughter, and immediately felt that he should have a chance. He mounted, was quickly thrown, and we had a truce. I got aboard again and walked him for the rest of the period.

Ontario remained my principal mount for my remaining days with the 11ᵗʰ Cavalry. [37] I finally cured him of cow kicking and he also became an adequate if not a willing jumper. He never really liked to be

---

[37] The 11ᵗʰ Cavalry Regiment later evolved into the modern 11ᵗʰ Armored Cavalry Regiment. Following its work in California, the regiment went on to see service in World War II, Vietnam, the Persian Gulf War, and the Wars in Iraq and Afghanistan.

saddled, particularly on cold nights and early dawns when the cinch was cold against his belly. He would extend his stomach until I had mounted and as soon as he relaxed I would reach down and tighten the cinch. One of his greatest moments came when in the field on a maneuver I galloped up to report to the squadron commander. I dismounted, saluted, and was promptly bitten on the butt. You could never take him for granted. Other horses deserving honorable mention include Bulldog, a biter but superb jumper; Kearney, who cow-kicked with either foot if you were foolish enough to stand close to his chest; Bad Eye, a really mean kicker who nevertheless was a fine pack horse; one of our kitchen packhorses who was docile enough when the kitchen pack was rapped heavily in burlap, but a real outlaw when someone forgot to muffle the sound of the pots; and Mercury, a great jumper who tended to run away in the excitement of it all unless you had him firmly under control.

I'll leave the horses with a mention of Heart-Bar-A, named for the brand on his hip. This horse, like so many, was a wonderful troop horse with one bad habit. He loved to buck when mounted, and was adept at throwing the uninitiated. Since he was in my platoon I felt that I should have a go at riding him. On a quiet Sunday morning, Wayne and I with a couple of interested troopers went down to the corral to saddle Heart-Bar for the bucking contest. We used a trooper's McClellan saddle with a five-pound grain feed sack to serve as a bucking roll, tied to the pommel. We blindfolded him and gingerly tightened the cinch. Trying not to show my trepidation I climbed aboard, took the reins in my left hand with my right aloft, and told them to remove the blindfold. He didn't bulge. I carefully touched him with the spurs and he moved out in a nice regulation walk. He never did explode. When I dismounted I felt that I had given him a chance to perform, and one was enough, I believe that the next day he quickly threw his assigned rider.

It was with mixed feelings that I left the horses on April 1, 1942. However, with war broken out I felt the irony of guarding the Mexican border with my horse platoon while tanks were overrunning Europe. At my request, I had been assigned to the 804th Tank Destroyer Battalion located at La Mesa, near San Diego and about 50 miles down the highway from Camp Lockett, which my regiment had built from scratch. My last act before driving to report to my new outfit was to go down to the corral to see Ontario for the last time. He was standing with the others, I called his name and he didn't move. Then I took some grain out to him and he took notice. I patted him, rubbed his neck, and said good bye and good luck. I left him dozing quietly in the sun.

Chapter 3

The Move to Tank Destroyers

ON the 6th day of January 1941, the War Department ordered into active duty Battery A, 158 Battalion, a New Mexico National Guard unit from Roswell, New Mexico. This unit had a record of five engagements in World War I. Shortly thereafter under the Army's gigantic expansion program, it was quickly converted into the 45th Infantry Division. Newly organized units from New Mexico soon joined it; a headquarters battery from Santa Fe, B battery from Raton, and C battery from Tucumcari. Lt. Col. Edward Purdy[38] of Roswell assumed command.

The battalion soon moved to Fort Sam Houston[39] for six months, conducting individual and small unit training while there; then later participated in the Louisiana-North Carolina Maneuvers for five months with the 1st Army in North Carolina and later the 3rd Army in Louisiana. At the outbreak of the war, the unit was rushed to the west coast, where at Camp San Luis Obispo, California,[40] it was reorganized in January, 1942, as the 804th Tank Destroyer Battalion. Three weeks in Camp San Luis Obispo and the newly organized Tank Destroyer Battalion moved to March Field, California[41] for three months, acting as airdrome security. It was around this time in April

---

[38] Texas native Edward Purdy (1901-1975) had prior to World War II commanded Battery A in the New Mexico National Guard. The unit had served honorably in The Philippines, Cuba, the Mexican border, and in World War I.

[39] Fort Sam Houston is a U.S. Army post located in San Antonio, Texas.

[40] Established in 1928, Camp San Luis Obispo is known as the original home of the California National Guard. It is located in San Luis Obispo County and is still in use today.

[41] Established in 1918, March Air Reserve Base (known during World War II as March Field) is one of the oldest airfields still operated by the U.S. Military. It is located near Moreno Valley, California.

1942 that I joined the 804th as commander of Company A. The next move for our battalion took us into the Desert Training Center[42] near Brawley, California, for a month's intensive training; then to La Mesa, California,[43] for two months training and coastal patrol. Here the Reconnaissance Company of the battalion was organized. The newly organized Tank Destroyer Center at Camp Hood, Texas,[44] was the next stopping place for the battalion, and two months were spent there training as a combat organization. Construction had just been started on the camp at this time, and the battalion moved into tents in the vicinity of Copperas Cove.[45] There were five battalions here in all at this time, the first group to train at the camp.

On July 29, 1942, our unit boarded the train to Gatesville, Texas—destination Indiantown Gap, Pennsylvania, a staging area.[46] Here all records for staging were probably broken; thirty-six hours after arriving, the battalion was entrained again and started en route for the New York Port of Embarkation. Formations were so fast and furious at Indiantown that one man was injected for typhus three times before he could get out of the line. August 6th found the unit on the Army transport *Thomas H. Barry*, with half of the men below decks and half above; every six hours there was a complete changeover. And then we hit some bad weather, to add to the discomfort of all. What a miserable trip that was—yes, war is hell. On the 17th of August we dropped anchor, at Belfast, Ireland. Here the battalion debarked and entrained for Camber, County Down—famous for its Irish whiskey. Sgt. Reed Van

---

[42]   The Desert Training Center (DTC) was a World War II-era training facility established in the Mojave Desert and Sonoran Desert, encompassing land in both southern California and western Arizona. Opened in 1942, it was a key training facility for units engaged in the 1942-1943 North African Campaign. While in operation, it was the largest military training ground in the history of military maneuvers. The DTC later closed in July 1944.

[43]   In operation from 1942 to 1944, Camp Le Mesa was an infantry battalion defense post and command center. It was located a few miles away from San Diego, California.

[44]   Camp Hood was re-named Fort Hood in 1950.

[45]   Copperas Cove is a small city located near Fort Hood, Texas.

[46]   Established in 1931, Fort Indiantown Gap is a U.S. Army post located in Lebanon County, Pennsylvania. During World War II, it was one of the nation's most important Army training camps and served as a staging area for the New York Port of Embarkation.

Wagenen,[47] an NCO in the 804th's Reconnaissance Company later wrote an excellent account of the battalion's activities during this period—I will include some of his reminiscences here. According to Reed:

> We were stationed outside a small town called Enniskillen, Northern Ireland, near the border of Southern Ireland, or the "Free State" as it was known. Our duty was to guard against the IRA (Irish Republican Army) of Southern Ireland. As far as I can remember, we did not have any trouble with them. We were told they came into Enniskillen, a few at a time, to eat and drink, but we never knew any of them. Maybe we drank with them at the pub—who knows?

There were many things to get accustomed to now—rain, shillings and pence, blackouts, right hand drive, rain, beer and skittles,[48] the Irish mile,[49] and more rain. The battalion was attached to the 34th Division here for training and administration. Physical conditioning was foremost on the program. After about two weeks at Camber the unit moved to Crom Castle,[50] near Newton Butler on the Irish border. It was the first castle most of us had seen, and a few days were spent on tours throughout the place. Battalion headquarters was set up in the castle, and Nissen huts[51] were used as barracks. According to Reed:

> The troops were housed in Quonset huts (sheet iron huts) that surround the castle. They were very comfortable and warm. The officers were assigned the huge castle for quarters. The castle was very beautiful... the grounds were green and

---

[47] A Utah native, Reed Van Wagenen (1912-1997) spent most of his adult life in the Los Angeles area. In the late 1980s, he and his wife self-published the account of his World War II service and gave a signed copy to Mr. Clement.

[48] "Beer and skittles" is a British expression for fun and leisure.

[49] The "Irish Mile" is the distance you can walk before passing out after a night of heavy drinking at the bar.

[50] Crom Castle has been home to the Crichton family, Earls of Earne for centuries. The Crichton family acquired the original castle in 1609 and built the present structure in 1820.

[51] A Nissen hut is a prefabricated steel structure, made from a half-cylindrical skin of corrugated steel. It was developed in World War I by inventor and British Army Major Peter N. Nissen and used extensively during World War II.

well kept, with trees and shrubbery all around. Surrounding Crom Castle was a moat with shrubs and small trees. The Captain had ordered guard duty around the officers' quarters in the castle, supposedly against the IRA... two guards were placed at each end of the castle, two would go this way, two would go that way. When they met each other, they'd yell "HALT—WHO GOES THERE!" at the top of their voices—every hour—all night long. They had those Lieutenants jumping and turning over all night. While stationed there, we were taken to an outside area to continue field training as well as playing football every other day and badminton in between. Later, we were sent for more commando training, only much harder than Fort Hood.

The next four months were spent in an intensive review of basic training, with a great amount of dismounted work. As Reed mentioned, a short term of guard duty broke up the routine for a little while. Equipment was not available for training with our primary weapon—the 75 mm gun mounted on the half-track. We had only a few jeeps and 37 mm guns on Fargo mounts, but we got a maximum of use from these vehicles. Then, late in November 1942, came the move to England—Stoke-on-Trent near Newcastle-under-Lynn. We quartered at Keele Hall; a large estate and residence turned over to the government for our use.[52] This was a most decided relief and a welcome change. There were several large towns in the neighborhood and passes were plentiful. London was only a few hours away by train. No, we won't forget our short stay in England. As Reed later reflected:

> England was severely rationed after the war years they had already suffered; any meat they could get was mixed with grain filler. They were generous and gracious in sharing what little they did have... The camp was abundant with food, so the fellows used to take some of the excess meat and sorely needed items to certain families... England was a beautiful place, much more American than our former place. The people there were much nicer to us; of course, they knew why we were there.

---

[52] Keele Hall was built around 1580 and later overhauled during the mid-19th century. In the early 20th century it was leased by Grand Duke Michael Mikhailovich of Russia (1861-1929). Following its use by the U.S. Army during World War II, it later became part of the Keele University campus.

You surely had to take your hat off to them the way they had to take it so long and yet keep in good spirits. Believe me, I've often wondered if we could take it over here like the average Englishman had it there.

Early in January 1943, an advance detail accompanied the 34th Division advance detail to Africa to prepare for the later arrival of the Battalion, and on 15th of January the Battalion sailed from England, arriving in Oran, Africa, 1st of February. As Reed reflected, we "were under then-Maj. Gen. George S. Patton's command, were moved inland and were used in some fringe action in that command and held in reserve for replacements in the operation taking place there at Kasserine Pass in central Tunisia." Most of the fringe action we were involved in involved night sentry duty. We were guarding captured German prisoners and their equipment, where it had been left, at a time when the enemy may have attempted to get those materials back. Anyway, who can forget our staging area outside of Oran—"Goat Hill"; and the first taste of fresh fruit in many months. Reed wrote at the time, "this camp almost went crazy last night after no mail for two months. They had mail call every half hour. It looked so funny to see everyone with Christmas packages out in the hot sunshine." Reed wrote further, "it's really a scream, all the heavy wool socks, sweaters and mufflers—what a place to get them! They can be worn at night, though!"

From "Goat Hill," the unit moved to "Mud Flats" about thirty miles from Oran. Here the battalion was attached to the 1st Tank Destroyer Group, bivouacking with the 813th and 894th Tank Destroyer Battalions. A few weeks here, and then the move to Chanzy, Algeria, about 90 miles away. Chanzy was probably the best training area we had seen. It was a beautiful spot, and not too far from Sidi-bel-Abbes, headquarters of the French Foreign Legion. We had had our equipment for several weeks now, and training was continued with new vigor. It was here that a cadre of Free French officers and enlisted men was sent to the battalion for training, and they proved to be apt pupils. Reflecting on this period, Reed also wrote:

You would get a big kick out of seeing all the Arab peddlers, coming out to our camp with practically anything and everything. We traded cigarettes with them for fresh oranges. I didn't realize I had missed them so much. I think I ate over a dozen the first day. Boy did they taste good! After the rain, snow and cold of Ireland and England, the desert sun also felt really good in February and March, but it was cold at night, so the fellows rigged up stoves to warm the larger tents with... necessity is the mother of invention alright. We took two 5-gallon cans, put them together; pieces of wood were put in the open end. The end with the open neck had metal flaps that could be lifted for draft or closed to hold heat. About 30 tomato cans, with a hole cut in each end, were stacked on top for a chimney. Throw a little gasoline on top of the wood, followed by a match—all the cans of the chimney would go plop-plop-plop, as they raised and lowered with the combustion. Anyway, you could warm one side at a time, which was a lot better than none. Meanwhile, a German propaganda broadcast played the best American swing records of any we heard. There was a girl with the sweetest voice that told us how sorry she felt for us, etc. Everyone got a big kick out of it. She tried to break everyone's morale, but instead we just enjoyed the music.

After a month in this area, under VI Corps, the unit moved further south to Sebdou, Algeria. Fifth Army was establishing a Tank Destroyer Training Center here, and the 804th was the first unit to attend. Meanwhile several officers and enlisted men left for an observation tour with units engaged in the fighting in Tunisia. Our advance party with the 34th Division returned and regaled us with tales of the early fighting in Tunisia, in which they had taken part. Then came the wind-up of the Tunisian campaign and with it thousands of Axis prisoners. This resulted for us in prisoner guard detail, and trips to England and back to the States, during July, August and September. According to Reed:

> By summer we were assigned to guard prisoners being returned to the U.S. on several "Kaiser Coffins," troop-carrying vessels. Italian prisoners were sent to England, German prisoners to the U.S. Some of the fellows said, "send them together; we won't have so many prisoners left." On July 30, 1943, we sailed from Oran to New York. Fifty or sixty prisoners were kept down in the hold of the ship. Twenty reconnaissance guards with sub-machine guns guarded them.
>
> Once a day, one of Recon's non-coms (without guns) accompanied by the two German non-coms, would go down into the hold to inspect the prisoners. The Germans kept their

quarters immaculately clean. German sergeants would take the food and distribute it. There was a latrine on each side of the ship, with one G.I. at each door of the hold and one at each latrine door with a sub-machine gun, to watch until the prisoner returned to the hold. While the ship was still leaving Oran and passing the north coast of Africa they had black-out drapes over everything. A prisoner could have struck a light when going to the latrine. Since there were still some scattered Nazi troops in the area, the U.S. soldiers were very watchful during that time; however, the prisoners didn't give them any problem. When the trip first started, the prisoners selected a spokesperson to ask where they were being shipped to. When the reply was the U.S., they were overjoyed because they knew the war was over for them. When the troop ship arrived in New York, the prisoners were taken to a nearby fort, where they were transferred to various prison camps in different states.

In October, 1943, the battalion was together again and back at the old camp site at Sebdou. Here instruction in artillery methods was reviewed. The routine was broken by frequent gazelle hunting expeditions near El Aricha, far to the south, and trips to Tlemcen, the nearest town of any size. However, as Reed reflected in his own account, G.I.'s had little luck hunting down the swift gazelles of North Africa. Although they tasted delicious, gazelles were usually so agile at zigzagging, and so fast, that they could outrun jeeps going at 50 miles an hour over rough terrain. In January 1944, the battalion was attached to the 88th Infantry Division commanded by Maj. Gen. John E. Sloan,[53] just recently arrived from the States and training at Magenta. The gun companies were made part of the RCT's for training purposes, and a thorough course in artillery methods supervised by Division Artillery was undertaken. The close contact with the infantry and artillery units of this division paid dividends later on when the unit went into combat with them. Each understood capabilities and limitations of the other, and a feeling of mutual trust and confidence sprang up which was never lost. We came to appreciate the fact that close contact and

---

[53] South Carolina native Maj. Gen. John E. Sloan (1887-1972) was a Class of 1910 U.S. Naval Academy graduate who commanded the 88th Infantry Division from July 1942 to September 1944.

knowledge of personalities in the units for which we worked insured teamwork and the best results.

However, North Africa also gave some of us our first taste of combat and foreshadowing of the difficult days that lay ahead. Reed was among the battalion's personnel who served as observers on the front lines and reflected on the experience as follows:

> They sent four of us Staff Sergeants to the front to "observe action" and learn first-hand what it was like in reality. We were sent in with the unit, issued the same weapons to defend ourselves with and were on our own to learn, and to stay alive. Until you get where the action is going on, you can't know how it feels to have the enemy trying to kill you. Actual live maneuvers against the enemy is a far cry from field maneuvers. Our commando training at Camp Hood, Texas seemed tough to us, coming into it from civilian life, but it was child's play compared to the real thing.... This phase of the war was over, but we were busy enough trying to learn new methods for the "big one."

"The big one" was an apt description for what laid ahead of us in Italy. We would quickly come to discover that it would be some of the most savage fighting of the entire war.

Chapter 4

Trial By Fire in Italy

THE 804th Tank Destroyer Battalion with the 88th Division Artillery embarked at Oran, Africa[54] on February 1, 1944, disembarking at Naples, Italy a week later. I was still a captain commanding Company A. We went into an initial tent camp bivouac area north of Naples a few miles. The enemy was dug in along the foothills of the Aurunci Mountains[55] and the Solacciano Ridge to Santa Maria Infante. Between our positions was a narrow valley less than half a mile wide. At that time the front line extended form Minturno[56] on the west coast to Ortona[57] on the east coast, 100 miles. Our bivouac area was an olive grove with a farmhouse nearby. We visited the family nightly, bringing rations in exchange for wine. They were happy to see the Americans and we all would gather in the kitchen by the big fireplace and attempt to learn basic Italian. "Dove Tedeschi" meant "Where are the Germans?" we were quick to learn; "Via, via" meant they were gone. One of the family, a little 10-year old girl had a beautiful voice and she introduced us to some of their songs; Pavarotti sings them today, including *Mama*, *Angelina*, *Non Ti Scordar di Me* (my favorite) and others. For example, she sang *Lili Marlene*, a German song, in Italian, and *J'Attendrai*, the French song, also. There was generally a guitar accompaniment and an accordion as well. Of course we (proba-

---

[54] Oran is the second largest city in Algeria.
[55] The Aurunci Mountains are located in the southern part of the Lazio Region of Italy
[56] Minturno is also located in the southern part of Italy's Lazio Region.
[57] Ortona is a coastal town in the Province of Chieti in Italy's Abruzzo Region. During World War II, it was the site of fierce fighting between German and Canadian forces. The ferocity of the battle led it to be later known as "Little Stalingrad." This Battle of Ortona lasted from December 20 to December 28, 1943.

bly me) introduced them to our songs. *Deep in the Heart of Texas* was a favorite.

It was a pleasant interlude prior to our moving up to a forward assembly area at Carinola, five miles from the front on March 5.[58] Here for the first time we could hear artillery fire in the distance. The Germans had limited air power meaning that air raids were possible. Blackout, foxholes, and cover positions were standard. We underwent no attack here but occasionally at night there was antiaircraft fire in the distance and the sound of a bomb or two. Limited training and inspection continued. General Sloan insured that there would be no let down in the combat zone. He had already indoctrinated us in Africa and we kept our areas clean, policed, and in good order. Daily maintenance on equipment was standard, to include ammunition and signal gear. Reconnaissance Company meanwhile departed for Mondragone[59] to act as beach patrol and to guard Minturno Bridge over the Garigliano.[60] By 9th of March A, B, and C Companies were in firing positions; A near Cello, B on the south bank of the Garigliano near its mouth, and C near Fasani. The following day C Company fired several rounds for registration and then threw 60 rounds of HE[61] at the enemy in a night harassing program. The battalion was in action!

I will never forget one inspection that took place shortly after we were committed. Reconnaissance Company, on the coast on the left flank had taken over a farmhouse for a command post. Only the first floor was used, the second being more vulnerable to enemy fire. General Sloan made an unannounced inspection and went directly to the second floor. Alas, the Germans had been using it as a latrine. In a rage, the division commander called our battalion commander back to headquarters and relieved him on the spot. A few incidents had taken place back in Africa and this was the last straw. It was a bad break for our commander, but a good break for me. Maj. Fred Rowell,[62] battal-

---

58 Carinola is located in Italy's Caserta Province.

59 Mondragone is also located in Italy's Caserta Province, located about 28 miles northwest of Naples.

60 The 25 mile long Garigliano River marks the boundary between the Italian Regions of Lazio and Campania.

61 "HE" stands for high explosive.

62 Fred G. Rowell (1912-1958) was a Pine Bluff, Arkansas native who resided for much of his life in Roswell, New Mexico, where he operated a jewelry store. He was active in the New Mexico National Guard before and after World War II and eventually reached the rank of brigadier general.

ion executive officer, was made commander and he named me as his replacement, a major's slot (when promoted). It was a relief to get away from this inspection routine once the offensive began. Sloan demanded a lot but he also got a lot in return. His was the first Selective Service Division in combat and it had a good reputation from the start.

Now back to the war. The 88th Division began relief of the British 5th Division on March 5. The German Gustav Line[63] extended north of the Garigliano River just beyond Minturno[64] on the west flank; the port of Gaeta, held by the enemy, could be seen across the gulf nine miles away. Their main line of resistance (MLR) was 3000 yards deep with dominating terrain features providing excellent observation of the coastal plain and Minturno area. The line swung north along the river to Cassino 15 miles away on the Rapido River and then on finally to Ortona on the east coast 100 miles away. The Hitler Line[65] was 15 to 20 miles away with its west flank at Fondi on the Appian Way (Highway 7) directly on the line of advance.

The division went in with three regiments abreast on a 10,000-yard front. The 350th Regiment was on the coast; the 351st in the center; and the 349th on the right. Critical terrain features held by the enemy included Santa Maria Infante on high ground opposite the 351st; the Ausente River Valley running north-south two miles to the east of Santa Maria; Mt. Daminao, a dominating feature on the right of the valley; and Castelforte, a beat up town to the east of Damiano.[66] The enemy positions on the Gustav Line were three to five miles deep in our sector. The battalion was committed with Company A supporting the 349th on the right, Company C with the 351st in the center, and Company B with the artillery on the coast. By March 9 all units were

---

[63] The Gustav Line was a heavily fortified German position that was built under the supervision of Field Marshal Albert Kesselring. The line was important strategically to the Allies because it had to be broken before Rome could be liberated.

[64] Minturno is a city in the southern part of Italy's Lazio region. Situated on the German Gustav Line during World War II, it suffered from heavy Allied bombing.

[65] The Hitler Line was a fallback position in case the Gustav Line was penetrated. It was later renamed the Senger Line after General Fridolin von Senger und Etterlin, who was one of the German generals commanding forces in the area. This was reportedly done at Hitler's insistence, in order to minimize any propaganda significance in case the line was penetrated.

[66] As part of the Gustav Line, Castelforte was also heavily damaged by Allied bombing during the Battles of Cassino between January and May 1944.

in position. Mt. Damiano and Castelforte absorbed a lot of Company A's fire, it being integrated with the artillery—some direct and some indirect.

Throughout the rest of March, April, and part of May, the big guns of the battalion threw thousands of rounds of HE at the enemy positions, disrupting lines of communication, knocking out their fortifications, and harassing them by day and night. Meanwhile Reconnaissance Company was busy patrolling the beaches and clearing mine fields. Headquarters Company, of course, had to attend to the needs of the battalion as a whole, supplying food, ammunition and fuel to the other companies within the battalion. The enemy was also busy, for several men were killed and wounded by the counter-battery dropped into the various company positions during this period.

Easter brought a surprise—rumors of a possible enemy tank attack down the Ausente River valley directly to our front. Brig. Gen. "Bull" Kendall,[67] Assistant Division Commander, appeared and asked how quickly the company could be in position facing the valley. "In half an hour," I said and was told to stand by. I immediately alerted the troops and shortly we got the order to move. What a scramble packing, loading, and getting ready to leave those now very familiar positions. I preceded the column by 15 minutes. This would be position selection on the run. About one half mile to our front we came to a small stream with what looked like a very substantial concrete arched bridge. I crossed, followed by the first TD.[68] The second vehicle caused the bridge to give way but not before the driver with good thinking quickly accelerated and just made it. I told Darrell Chandler, my executive officer to take another route a couple of miles to the right. Meanwhile, I found a couple of positions and prepared to spend the night. We were in no-man's land and I expected to meet an enemy patrol at any moment but the night was uneventful. The rest of the company arrived at dawn and got into firing positions blocking the valley. The tank attack was a false alarm but we remained in these forward positions, extending about a mile. A 24-hour guard was maintained and I checked all

---

[67] Paul W. Kendall (1898-1983) was a Kansas and Wyoming native who graduated from West Point in 1918. He later commanded the 88th Infantry Division from September 1944 to July 1945 and was commander of I Corps during the Korean War. He retired from the Army in 1955 with the rank of lieutenant general.

[68] "TD" stands for tank destroyer.

positions daily beginning at the crack of dawn. This led to the court martial of a platoon leader whose crew was asleep when I checked in.

Let me tell you now about how we came to operate generally. The battalion provided (1) direct fire support at specific or suspected targets pointed out by infantry troops or by our own destroyer commanders or others in a position to observe; (2) indirect fire support from artillery positions in rear of the front line units. A typical battalion deployment might be one company in support of a front line regiment; another supporting an adjacent unit; and the third firing with the artillery. As the executive officer, I operated usually with one of the front line companies in addition to supervising logistic operations—resupply for example. When supporting these various units we were under their operational command: Go there and do that. I interpreted my job to be to ensure that the mission was appropriate and that we got the job done. The terrain was difficult for armor, being mountainous with limited roads and opportunity for maneuver. It meant painstaking foot reconnaissance to find the trail that led to a good firing position. The basic idea was to have that big three-inch gun bring accurate fire on the enemy positions, known or suspected; holding up the advance.

The Tank Destroyer School would not have recognized our TDs in combat. The January trip to Italy by a few of us gave us a chance to spend combat time with our counterparts held up at Cassino. We brought back ideas for company identification markings, striped gun barrels for example, improvised sandbag tops for our open turrets; attached metal carrying frames for extra equipment. This gear would be dropped off prior to a front line engagement. A unit on the road was a sight to behold, carrying extra rations—potatoes, tomatoes, corn and even chickens liberated from the countryside.

Mail was important and we got it in intervals. Each company had a mail orderly and these soldiers took great pride in seeing that the mail "got through" combat or not, crawling the last few yards to a firing gun position if necessary. All outgoing mail was censored by company officers. No identifiable locations or events could be described. This led to a lot of weather and family talk and some complaining of course. But once in combat there was less of the latter. I wrote home about once a week using standard V-mail to let them know I was OK.

The medics deserve special mention. They took care of the wounded at all costs, crawling under fire to give first aid and getting the casualty back to the aid station. The communications men were also good, repairing ripped up telephone wire under mortar or artillery fire, insuring that vital communications were restored. And what about those engineers—clearing mines, building bridges and improvising detours, a lot of this also under fire. You saw the value of the combined arms team very quickly in combat and got to appreciate the contribution of each member.

The battalion was already experienced in breaking camp and moving out in good order having been activated back in 1941. On getting orders to move we would immediately send out liaison to the units to be supported. Our own battalion advance party, perhaps myself and the S-3 operations officer and a jeep-load of guides, would precede the main body by 30 minutes. We carried battalion sign markers to indicate the direction to be taken, with guides left at critical points. You can imagine the difficulty of this maneuver at night with blackout lights. I am still amazed at some of those moves. One in particular in October 1944 was a masterpiece. We got orders at dusk to join the 91st Division [69] a few miles to the east. The order of march was given, the advance detail left and away we went. We arrived at our assembly area a few hours later, in pitch dark, and checked the companies in. There had been no hitch but somehow all of Company B got ahead of Company C with no real disorder or lost detachments. We had a good outfit. They could do it all. Our attitude under Fred was positive and we strove to accomplish the mission. The infantry appreciate it when they see you out there with them under fire.

One of the first things to get used to was being under enemy mortar and artillery fire. Their positions were generally 500 to a few thousand yards away masked by high ground. The Germans were masters at picking defensive positions with good observations and fields of fire. Our engineers had smoke pots going at bridge sites and road junctions that were otherwise in plain view. It was an anxious feeling knowing that you were under enemy eyes as you moved around. Nearer the front the risk was greater. My first exposure to artillery fire was shortly after we were committed and a big-caliber artillery round landed in the vicinity. There was a high pitched whirring sound and then the crash and the sound of fragments flying by. The sound was unmistakable and gave you about a second to hit the ground. Outgoing made a different sound but it took a while before we stopped ducking all artillery. Mortars were a different story. They were the infantryman's artillery with short range and soundless. Their crunch when they landed

---

[69] Attached to the U.S. Fifth Army, the 91st Division fought exclusively in Italy during World War II and was sometimes called the "Pine Tree Division" or the "Wild West Division."

was particularly nerve-shaking. The infantryman thinks that anything behind his mortars is rear echelon.

May 1, 1944 brought my executive officer assignment with Fred Rowell taking command of the battalion. I vowed that any company need or complaint would be met. *Ah youth*, to quote one of my favorite authors, Joseph Conrad.[70] As a company commander, I had felt that no one at battalion level seemed to be listening. And now, a seasoned veteran, I reflect on how consistently we seemed to wonder how the boss ever made it. Ah well, I tried; I listened, took notes and followed up. Fred agreed that we would both stress the operational mission and rely on the staff to handle administration and supply. It worked and pleased me greatly since I could then visit the companies and go where the action was, insuring that we were carrying out assigned missions and also being supported properly.

I felt that I should get to see how the platoon leaders functioned, they with their noncoms being so essential to our performance. We operated in a decentralized fashion with companies supporting infantry regiments and platoons in turn assigned down to battalions and even companies. It was essential that we understood our missions and also that the infantry understood our capabilities and limitations. A novice platoon leader might be guilty of dragging his feet in carrying out his mission. We did not want that. I think I can say now that we earned a good reputation in combat for getting the job done. Our direct fire support with that fine three-inch gun was a great morale builder for a front-rank rifleman whose protection was his shirt. And so I got to know the command and am grateful to Fred for letting me operate in this way. Very quickly you learned who needed supervision and whom you could trust to do the job.

The men go where led. It is essential to have a strong NCO and officer chain of command—courageous and with initiative. We weeded out those who couldn't lead. And on that score we also recommended about 20 of our platoon sergeants for promotion to second lieutenant. This was done. The actual wording of the promotion order has a nice ring to it: "...having clearly demonstrated their fitness for promotion by outstanding performance in actual combat..." As a company commander, I was very proud to see Morris Snow,[71] Clarence Troeger,[72]

---

[70] That quote appeared in Joseph Conrad's (1857-1924) autobiographical short story, "Youth," which was written in 1898.

[71] Morris H. Snow (1919-2010) was a Dallas, Texas native who grew up in Roswell, New Mexico. Along with his battlefield commission to second

continued...

and Byrel Moore,[73] all good New Mexicans, get combat appointments. I see them at our reunions in Roswell, New Mexico where we discuss our aches and pains. None of us could pass a physical for combat today.

Finally on 11 May at 2300 hours, the great artillery barrage began and the 804th Tank Destroyer Battalion joined in with the Long Toms,[74] the 240mm Howitzers, 105's and 75's, pouring tens of thousands of rounds of HE at the enemy position—the long awaited attack had begun! As the infantry regiments moved forward under the protective covering of the barrage, the firing companies of the battalion quickly moved up for direct fire support of the infantry regiments to which they had been attached—Company A supporting the attack of the 349th Infantry Regiment, Company B for indirect firing missions, attached to the 338th FA Battalion, Company C supporting the attack of the 351st Infantry Regiment with one platoon alerted to repel a possible hostile armored attack. Meanwhile Reconnaissance Company, with the exception of one platoon, was sent forward with the firing companies for reconnaissance and liaison work. The 3rd platoon of Reconnaissance Company, with three 81mm mortars, was attached to the 350th Infantry Regiment for support. Once the attack had begun there could be no let up.

The first enemy air attack I experienced was a night or two after the May 11 jump off. We had overall air superiority but the enemy could launch a few sporadic night attacks. One did this so regularly

---

...continued

lieutenant, Snow also earned a Bronze Star and Purple Heart for his service with the 804th Tank Destroyer Battalion in Italy. After the war, he served as a bookkeeper for Savage Brothers Electric in Roswell for 38 years before retiring with his wife Audrey to California in 2004. In retirement, he was also active in planning reunions for the 804th.

[72] Clarence E. Troeger (1914-2004) was a Kansas native who spent most of his life living in New Mexico and California. Following his World War II service, he was discharged from the U.S. Army as a first lieutenant and worked for the U.S. Postal Service in Santa Monica, California. He spent his retirement in Ruidoso, New Mexico.

[73] Byrel A. Moore (1918-2009) was a longtime Albuquerque, New Mexico resident who also served in the U.S. Army during the Korean War. Following his military service, he worked for Safeway Grocery Stores until his retirement in 1979.

[74] The Long Tom was a 155 millimeter caliber field gun used by the U.S. Army during World War II and the Korean War.

that we called him Bed Check Charlie. We were located in a farmhouse kitchen about to bed down when we heard anti-aircraft fire and then a screeching sound increasing in intensity and seemingly coming right down on us. We hit the floor when the bomb hit about 100 yards away—close enough to keep us down for a while. Luck plays a big part in combat as elsewhere. For some reason, I always felt that the other fellow was at risk and not me; I believe that a lot of us felt this way. It seems to me that motivation under fire derives from a feeling for your immediate group, your fellow soldiers. If they were in trouble you help, and they help you. Personal attachment to the unit means a lot.

An emerging combat situation can get the adrenalin flowing however, and supply its own motivation. The enemy becomes a personal thing to be dealt with and brings total concentration and even anger that those SOBs think they can prevail. Individual exploits above and beyond the call result.

The Fifth Army built up for the attack in the early days of May. Supply depots were stocked to insure plentiful ammunition, food, and fuel. MPs were brought in to control unauthorized traffic, maintain blackout conditions, cover windshields on jeeps to prevent sun reflection, and to ensure that helmets were worn. The 85th Division was committed to its first action on the coast to the left of the 88th Division. These two Selective Service divisions comprised the US 11 Corps. A French Corps was on the right, including Moroccan and Algerian Divisions, plus three groups of Tabors (Goumiers). [75] The latter were Berbers, skilled mountain fighters, whose weapons included knives and swords. Called "Gooms," they were feared by the Germans because they gave no quarter.

The attack was controlled by a series of objectives designed to penetrate the Gustav Line, and by well-defined terrain features serving as unit flank boundaries. Initial objectives were followed by subsequent ones for penetration to the enemy rear echelon, and headed north to Rome. These objectives were critical terrain features; hill masses, road junctions, villages, and even cemeteries with their walls affording cover. Objectives were defended in strength on the main line of resistance (MLR) and less so between subsequent lines. The Germans had con-

---

[75] The Moroccan Goumiers were indigenous soldiers who served in auxiliary units attached to the French Army of Africa between 1908 and 1956. While nominally in the service of the Sultan of Morocco, they served primarily under French officers. The Goumiers served in Italy and then France between 1942 and 1945.

structed the Hitler Line 20 miles away, running through Fondi on Highway 7. Typically, they would leave a third or less of their force to conduct delaying action while the main body continued on. Movement in the forwarded areas was at night in deference to our air superiority.

D-Day, H-Hour was 11:00 PM (2300) on 11 May. A tremendous artillery and mortar barrage started the show. Company A was supporting the 350th with direct fire opposite the Ausente River valley and Mt. Damiano on the right. Company B was attached to an artillery battalion for indirect fire support. Company C was supporting the 351st with direct fire against the strongest point in the line—Santa Maria Infante. The boundary between leading regiments was marked by 40-mm tracer fire from antiaircraft vehicles, a very wise idea. As the infantry moved forward slowly, our battalion's destroyers followed closely, neutralizing enemy machine gun nests, blasting at strong points, and smashing the enemy at every possible chance. Company A soon moved forward to the vicinity of Hill 100, Ceracoli, and Cerri to support an armored attack up the Ausente River; Company B had been called out of their indirect fire positions and was also supporting the drive near Cerri; C Company was supporting a tank and infantry attack towards Castellonotato from the vicinity of Santa Maria Infante. Reconnaissance Company moved out of observation posts near Castelforte and Domiano and acted as liaison between the infantry and our battalion, moving forward with the infantry.

Mt. Damiano was taken. Company A supported a tank battalion attack up the river valley at dawn. The 351st hit stubborn resistance at Santa Maria, the enemy on high ground with clear fields of fire, well-constructed emplacements, and a few buildings all enabling covering fire from left and right. This was a key point in the Gustav Line defenses, typically assigned to Colonel Champeny's[76] 351st Regiment to crack. Our Company C did good work delivering precision fire over pinned down infantry, including pinpoint fire through specific windows as designated. Enemy mortar and artillery fire was heavy in re-

---

[76] Arthur S. Champeny (1893-1979) was a Wisconsin native who served with distinction in World War I, World War II, and Korea. He is the only American to have earned the Distinguished Service Cross in three different wars and was severely wounded during the Korean War. Champeny retired from the U.S. Army in 1953 as a brigadier general and later settled in Kansas.

turn. Colonel Champeny was fearless.[77] On a few occasions, in Civil War style, he calmly walked out in plain view to exhort his troops. My friend and classmate Vic Hobson was the regimental executive officer.[78] I see him occasionally now, rather ill. We don't swap war yarns. The 351st was one of the best so it got the tough missions.

The 85th Division was committed on the coast on the left of the 88th; Company B supported their 338th Regiment. The division did quite well in its first action, taking its initial objective, a low mass hill, on schedule. The division Selective Service gamble was paying off. The coastal sector included Highway 7, the old Appian Way, and direct road to Anzio, and Rome.

Santa Maria fell on 14 May and the Gustav line was broken! The 351st continued toward the Hitler Line through very rough and hilly terrain for about two miles. Meanwhile the 349th took its initial objectives—Bracchi and Cerri—two miles beyond the MLR. The 350th took its objectives, including Mt. Rotondo, staying up with the 349th. By May 21, the Hitler Line was broken concluding phase two of the operation. The 88th line extended from Pico on the right to Itri[79] five miles from the coast. The 85th had made good progress on the left taking the old port of Gaeta[80] and Sperlonga[81] seven miles beyond. Obviously the

---

[77] Then-Colonel Champeny's second DSC citation reads as follows: "The President of the United States takes pleasure in presenting a Bronze Oak Leaf Cluster in lieu of a Second Award of the Distinguished Service Cross to Arthur S. Champeny (0-8264), Colonel (Infantry), U.S. Army, for extraordinary heroism in connection with military operations against an armed enemy while serving with the 351st Infantry Regiment, 88th Infantry Division, in action against enemy forces from 11 to 14 May 1944. Colonel Champeny's outstanding leadership, personal bravery and zealous devotion to duty exemplify the highest traditions of the military forces of the United States and reflect great credit upon himself, the 88th Infantry Division, and the United States Army."

[78] Victor W. Hobson (1918-2000) was an Alabama native who graduated with Clement from West Point in 1940. He served in the U.S. Army until 1965 and retired at the rank of brigadier general. Hobson later did defense consulting work in the Washington D.C. area until fully retiring in 1991.

[79] Itri is a small city in Italy's Latina Province. During World War II, Allied bombing destroyed 75 percent of the city's edifices.

[80] Today, Gaeta is home to a large NATO naval base. It is also used as the home port for the flagship of the United States' Sixth Fleet.

[81] Situated in Italy's Latina Province, Sperlonga is located about halfway between Rome and Naples.

main defenses were in the hills overlooking the coast. Fondi on Highway 7 was taken by a reconnaissance force and represented a three-mile salient beyond the Itri-Sperlonga line. Sixteen miles in ten days—good going in very difficult conditions.

The battalion continued supporting the regiments but it was not good armor terrain. The highway provided access to side roads into the hills. Supply was difficult, with Highway 7 used as the base from which company vehicles operated. Battalion headquarters was on the highway near Itri. Here I experienced my second air attack. We were bunked down in a barn, with cots and mosquito netting, the latter together with atabrine tablets being our main defense against malaria.[82] We heard bombs in the vicinity—coming closer. The barn offered some protection and we stayed put and I'm sure prayed. But Herb Lowery, a staff member, got excited and ran outside clad only in shorts. We heard the crunch when he slipped in the mud outside. A bedraggled Lowery came back to the derision of the staff. The attack was over.

The Anzio landings had occurred on January 22, 1944 with VI Corps, 60 miles beyond the Gustav Line. VI Corps established a bridgehead 10 miles deep, short of Cisterna, under enemy observation and fire; but no further progress had been made after the landing.[83] A link-up with II Corps was eagerly looked for. The VI corps commander, Maj. Gen. Lucian Truscott[84] ordered an attack on May 23, with II Corps elements 18 miles away. Two British divisions plus the 45th, 3rd, and 1st Armored Divisions led the attack, with the 34th and 36th coming in later. Key objectives, Cisterna and Cori were taken in two days and a link-up occurred.

Meanwhile the 88th Division continued the attack beyond the Gustav Line, in the hill masses overlooking the coast and Highway 7. The battalion supported the advance: with the 349th to Mt. Passigano

---

[82] Atabrine (also known as Mepacrine) was used extensively by the U.S. Armed Forces during World War II as an antimalarial drug.

[83] During the Battle of Cisterna in January/February 1944, roughly 96% of the city's buildings were destroyed. The city was largely rebuilt in the 1970s.

[84] Gen. Lucian K. Truscott Jr. (1895-1965) successively commanded the 3rd Infantry Division, VI Corps, U.S. Fifteenth Army and U.S. Fifth Army during World War II. He was, therefore, the only American officer to command a division, a corps, and a field army on active service during the war.

NOTHING IMPOSSIBLE

east of Fondi;[85] with the 350th through Fondi and then northwest to Mt. Cassarcio; with the 351st meeting heavy resistance back at Itri. The attack continued northwest to the hill towns of Rotondo (349th) and Rocassseca (350th). These little country villages were situated in the sparse road network through the hill country and were natural delaying positions for the withdrawing Germans. They were also prime targets for our three-inch guns pointed out by the advancing infantry. The 28th of May found lead elements of the 88th at the Amaseno River line, headed toward Highway 6. The enemy was routed, leaving delaying forces and heading for the Gothic Line[86] defenses about 100 miles away. The terrain favored his rear guard action, with a limited road network through hilly and mountainous country.

June 2 found VI Corps on Highway 7 approaching Rome through the Alban hills. On the right was II Corps, Lt. Gen. Geoffrey Keyes[87] commanding, heading for Highway 6 and then to Rome. The battalion was with the 88th Division, with the 85th on the left and the 3rd on its right, 10 miles from Rome in the Alban hills. Rome had been declared an open city but resistance remained on the outskirts. In fact, the Alban hills formed a part of the Caesar Line defenses.[88] It became increasingly evident now that the enemy would not be able to offer more than delaying action between our positions and Rome. The 351st was south of Valmontone[89] on Highway 6 on May 31. The going had been slow with no roads for tracked vehicles. The highway provided good going and we got on it to link up later with the 88th. Task Force Howze from the 1st Armored Division was leading the II Corps advance into Rome. Progress on the highway was held up by enemy armor and air. I was with Company B following the task force but still

---

[85] Located in Italy's Latina Province, Fondi is situated roughly halfway between Rome and Naples.

[86] Built under the supervision of Field Marshall Albert Kesselring, the Gothic Line was the last major German line of defense along the summits of the northern part of the Apennine Mountains during their fighting retreat from the Allies. As with the Hitler Line, Hitler demanded that it be renamed to minimize propaganda significance in case the line was breached. It was therefore later renamed the Green Line.

[87] Lt. Gen. Geoffrey Keyes (1888-1967) commanded the U.S. Army's II Corps during the Italian Campaign in World War II.

[88] The Caesar Line was the last German line of defense before Rome during the Italian Campaign in World War II.

[89] Located in Italy's Rome Province, Valmontone is located approximately 28 miles southeast of Rome.

attached to the 88th Division. Colonel Howze[90] requested flank protection against German armor in order to move on. I said we would give it, figuring that the 88th would not fault our effort to speed the advance. It worked out and I continued on with Company B, picking out a command post at Pallarium, a few miles east of Rome and on the highway. Rome was in sight and we felt elated.

The battalion started moving rapidly up Highway 2 towards Rome and on the 4th of June, 1944, its leading elements entered the Eternal City! Orders from the 88th were to join the 351st at three bridges over the Tiber at dawn. This would ensure an advance in pursuit of the retreating enemy. The bridges included the Ponte Milvio[91] and the Ponte Puca, and I felt that I could find them with the help of a good map which I had. The Company B commander was all for trying to find the bridges at dawn. I felt we should get moving and not waste time since it was getting dark. Fred Rowell agreed and I said I would lead the column, determined to be with the infantry at dawn.

The map was good and the route followed main avenues without many detours. It was now dark with sporadic shooting in the city but no real resistance. My driver and I led the 12 TDs, the lead vehicle with that big gun almost overhead. We wound our way through the historic city finally arriving at our objective after midnight. I went forward to find the infantry commander and he was glad to have our guns on hand. There had been a firefight at a bridge earlier, friendly fire. A detachment of the 1st Special Service Force had crossed the bridge earlier, unbeknownst to the approaching infantry who took them under fire; a lack of communication, but finally straightened out. Company B was now in good shape ready to continue on with the 351st, the latter riding the TDs in some cases.

---

[90] Hamilton H. Howze (1908-1998) was the son of Medal of Honor recipient and West Point Commandant Maj. Gen. Robert L. Howze. He graduated from West Point in 1930 and commanded the 1st Armored Division in Italy between 1944 and 1945. Howze was later a developer and advocate of helicopter-borne air mobility warfare. He retired from the U.S. Army at the rank of general in 1965 and was later an executive with Bell Helicopter in Fort Worth, Texas.

[91] The Milvian Bridge (*Ponte Milvio* in Italian) is a bridge over the Tiber River in northern Rome. It was an economically and strategically important bridge in the era of the Roman Empire and was the site of the famous Battle of the Milvian Bridge in 312 AD.

The taking of Rome meant headlines in our overseas paper, *Stars and Stripes*. The Normandy landings two days later put us on the back page from then on. But we had our Bill Mauldin[92] and his wonderful cartoons; "Is there a view for the enlisted men?" queries a just-joined second lieutenant. The advance continued north on Highway 52 and then Highway 3. I picked our first command post just north of the city; the Villa Climenti, a one night stay; a huge villa beautifully situated with a huge master bedroom. I slept there briefly, boots and all. Then off at dawn. By June 5, a bridgehead had been established about five miles north of Rome. The 88th was to advance with three regiments abreast, using a secondary road network and slow progress. Some of the forward units were truck and tank mounted. Our battalion was attached to the Ellis Task Force with a tank battalion and a reconnaissance squadron, trying to advance rapidly after the fleeing enemy. This was not good armor country and the force was road bound—about three miles long. The general mission was to screen the 88th Division as it advanced. Highway 3, which ran north-south along the Tiber, was now saturated with armor.

---

[92] William H. Mauldin (1921-2003) was a two-time Pulitzer Prize-winning journalist most famous for his World War II cartoons depicting American soldiers, as represented by the archetypal characters "Willie" and "Joe."

Chapter 5

Hard Fighting Against the Germans

THE next major German delaying position would be about 55 miles north of Rome, from Nunziatelle on the west coast to Viterbo,[93] Lake Bracciano,[94] and Orte[95] on the Tiber. The towns were choke points on the advance and were heavily defended. Resistance was slight between towns. A lack of opposition leads to carelessness. For example, the lead unit of our force included a kitchen truck, hoping to make the march unopposed and thus have a hot meal when the troops rolled in. A bad decision because the truck was hit with a bazooka; the war was over for the kitchen crew. It's a deadly game and carelessness kills.

About June 8, 1944, I was with the lead elements entering Orte. There was a narrow road leading down to the town, under enemy observation and fire. Infantry units had slipped to the right and entered the town on the far side. We would be supporting them. As I came up a discussion was being held by tank and TD platoon commanders as to who should lead. I solved it very practically by flipping a coin. The order of march had tanks and TDs alternating down this narrow trail; I followed the lead in my jeep. We took some fire but made it without incident. The tactical decision in this case was up to the supported infantry who were not in the vicinity. We fanned out on a road on the edge of town. I was about to start through the town to contact the infantry when a German machine gun opened up from a farmhouse about 50 yards away. I hit the ground and a TD swung its big gun around and fired point blank through the window; end of engagement.

---

[93] Located in Italy's Lazio region, Viterbo is approximately 50 miles north of Rome.

[94] Lake Bracciano is a lake of volcanic origin located approximately 20 miles northwest of Rome.

[95] Located in Italy's Viterbo Province, Orte is approximately 37 miles north of Rome and 15 miles east of Viterbo.

I walked through the quiet town with the tank commander to contact the infantry. The Italians had left or were hiding. When contact was made, I told of our covering position on the high ground. Enemy mortar and artillery fire were hitting intermittently on the infantry positions on the edge of town and the advance was halted for the time being. I returned to our guns deployed in a field and facing hostile ground on a ridge about 1000 yards away. I directed our guns to shoot at suspected strong or observation points, such as church steeples. Also, our fire would cause the enemy to give his attention to us with our armor protection rather than to the shirt-clad doughboy.

And so we opened up taking the opposing ridge complete with church under fire. We drew fire as expected. I had a close call here running from one TD to the next when a round came in landing so close that the black smoke drifted over and fragments went whistling by, one landing on me. One of the men thought I had been hit but I was lucky.

From here we had a respite at a rest area at Lake Albano[96] south of Rome. The 88th also came out of the line. A welcome rest and a chance to regroup, perform maintenance, change clothes and shower. These latter facilities were at various locations provided by the quartermaster. While at Alban, General Sloan had a commanders' call to critique the operation to date. He pulled no punches but in general gave compliments for a job well done. The 351st and Colonel Champeny got special praise. The tank destroyers came in for praise as well, with General Sloan noting that they were in action wherever he happened to be. Quite a compliment from a very exacting commander. A kind word goes a long way and we were certain that the word got down to the men who were responsible.

On June 23 the battalion moved to Follinica[97] on the coast, 10 miles from the front, and attached to the 34th Division veterans of the African campaign. The enemy was holding the Lake Trasimeno Line, 50 miles from the Arno River and the historic city of Florence. The port of Piombino[98] had been taken and the major port of Livorno

---

[96] Lake Albano is a small volcanic crater lake at the foot of Monte Cavo in Lazio, located approximately 12 miles southeast of Rome. The Papal Palace of Castel Gandolfo (the Pope's summer residence), is located in the area.

[97] Follinica is located about 25 miles northwest of the city of Grosseto in Italy's Tuscany region.

[98] Piombino is a small town in Italy's Tuscany region.

NOTHING IMPOSSIBLE

(Leghorn) was 40 miles up the coast. The line had advanced 30 to 40 miles from June 10 when the battalion had been relieved. The enemy had offered resistance all the way. Our battalion had Companies A, B, and C with the 168th, 135th, and 133rd Regiments of the 34th. June 30 found the 133rd and Company C at heavily defended Cecina.[99] A German counterattack was mounted—tanks and infantry—across the fields on the coast, headed for the town. They approached and then a platoon of Company C opened up and stopped them. They scattered and Cecina was secured later on July 1. I remember thinking that this was the most explosive July 4 I had ever experienced. At one point I was ducking around a building and bumped into another party coming the other way. We both jumped and then discovered that we were classmates—Herb Bowlby.[100] We were later at the War College together.

We were quite proud to be given the coastal zone of advance by the 34th Division on July 10, operating on the left flank of the division. It was not the norm for a TD battalion, but we were a pretty good outfit. We had a task force which included the battalion plus the 34th and 91st Reconnaissance Troops. Rosignano Solvay[101] had been taken on the coast but Rosignano Martina on high ground to the east was holding up the 168th Infantry. Leghorn, a major port was 15 miles away.[102] Castiglioncello[103] was taken by the battalion on July 12. This was a pretty little resort on the coast. I rode in an armored car with our reconnaissance unit down broad, shallow steps that led to the quay,[104] across the plaza and up steps on the far side. It would be a nice

---

[99] The ancient town of Cecina, located in Italy's Tuscany region, was totally destroyed during World War II. From the 1960s onwards, it was redeveloped as a popular tourist resort.

[100] Herbert M. Bowlby, Jr. (1918-1995) of Pennsylvania served as a major in the 517th Parachute Regimental Combat Team during World War II and was a recipient of the Bronze Star. He retired from the U.S. Army with the rank of colonel.

[101] Located in Tuscany, Rosignano Solvay is famous for its white beaches, whose sand is formed by limestone and calcium chloride produced by the nearby Solvay since 1914.

[102] Leghorn is the English name for the Italian city of Livorno. It is the capital of the Italian Province of Livorno in the Tuscany region.

[103] Located in Tuscany, Castiglioncello has been a renowned sea resort since the 19th century.

[104] A quay is a concrete, stone, or metal platform lying alongside or projecting into water for loading and unloading ships.

place to visit someday. We occupied a ridge north of town opposed by enemy on a facing ridge; Leghorn was now a few miles away. It was here I planned an armor attack on the opposing ridge. It was apparent that the Germans had a screening force, the main opposition being on the high ground to our right where the infantry was slowly advancing. I received the Bronze Star Medal for Valor for this action. [105]

An infantry force was to join us on the ridge but they didn't make it. Pinned down they said. Nonsense I said. We had to pull back since infantry would be needed to secure the position with us overnight. A German counterattack could be expected but it didn't happen. We had already used an engineer platoon a day or so earlier to tactically set up a defensive perimeter with us, we having taken quite a chunk of ground. The engineers were eager but we caught it from division for this supposed misuse of engineers. War is like that, but we had done the right thing. As we pulled back, the M8 [106] that I was on ran into a ditch. The driver had his head down ducking I don't know what. I jumped off, unhooked the tow cable and hooked it on to another M8 to pull us out. It worked, but I still remember feeling that we were prime targets while this was going on.

Castiglioncello has fond memories for me because I was promoted to major here on July 15, 1944. A combat appointment as it is called in Army orders: "having clearly demonstrated...fitness for promotion by outstanding performance in actual (sic) combat..." This was a temporary promotion. The Regular Army list moved much more slowly; it would be another eight years before that promotion came. But I immediately had the rank and pay. A good friend and classmate, Frank Meszar, [107] was visiting me from an Air Corps unit to the south. We had a great celebration that night, wine all around. Another thing to be

---

[105] Refer to Appendix D for the full citation of this Bronze Star decoration.

[106] The 75 mm Howitzer Motor Carriage M8, also known as the M8 Scott, was a self-propelled U.S. Army howitzer vehicle developed during World War II. It was used primarily in the Italian Campaign, the Western Front, and the Pacific Theater of Operations.

[107] Frank Meszar (1915-2002) was a Georgia native and 1940 West Point graduate who served in World War II, Korea, and Vietnam. He began his military career as an infantry officer but later became a renowned helicopter pilot and aviation school commander. Meszar retired from the U.S. Army in 1970 at the rank of brigadier general. His son, Capt. Frank Meszar III (1944-1969), was killed in action in Vietnam.

proud of was the bulge in the division situation map indicating the front line, ahead of the 34th Division on our right.

We regrouped and sent patrols to verify a German withdrawal. Late on July 17 following one of our patrols we started for Leghorn. We entered the city early next morning. Meanwhile, our Company C had come in with lead elements of the 168th riding their TDs. A celebration ensued for a while. Quite a bit of wine had been liberated and five-gallon cans were being filled. On July 22, my birthday, we rejoined the 88th Division and moved up 10 miles to Pisa [108] on the Arno River. Florence was about 40 miles east, also on the Arno. The south bank of the river became the new front line. River crossing training ensued—Companies A, B, and C being attached to the 349th, 350th and 351st respectively.

During June three veteran divisions—3rd, 36th, 45th—had been withdrawn to prepare for the Southern France landings with the Seventh Army (15 August). This meant a boundary shift to the west for the British Eighth Army, giving the U.S. Fifth Army a 30-mile front along the Arno; IV Corps [109] on the left (23 miles) and II Corps on the right with the 85th, 88th, and the 91st Divisions on a seven mile front, and 18 miles west of Florence. Training was a welcome respite from the continuous assault beginning May 11. But this pause on the Arno also provided the enemy time to strengthen his Gothic Line defenses 25 miles away, as we found out later.

The Germans evacuated Florence on August 2 and British Indian troops entered on the 13th. Two days later, the Seventh Army landed in Southern France. August 20 found the battalion attached to the 91st Division training at Volterra [110] 25 miles south of the Arno and 35 miles southwest of Florence. On the 26th, we moved up to

---

[108] Located in Tuscany, Pisa is best known for its famous leaning tower (a free standing bell tower of the city's cathedral). During World War II, the Allies discovered that the Germans were using the tower as an observation post. A U.S. Army sergeant sent to confirm the presence of German troops in the tower was impressed by the beauty of the cathedral and its campanile, and thus refrained from ordering an artillery strike, sparing it from destruction.

[109] IV Corps was reconstituted on 27 June 1944, replacing the VI Corps in the U.S. Fifth Army's order of battle in the Italian campaign, after Allied forces liberated Rome in the summer of 1944 when VI Corps was withdrawn to take part in Operation Dragoon, the Allied invasion of southern France.

[110] Volterra is an ancient Roman town located in Tuscany.

Grassina.[111] September 1 found the battalion supporting the 88th (B and C Companies) and the 91st (A and Reconnaissance Companies) Divisions. An unopposed river crossing was made on September 3, just east of the city. I remember seeing the Ponte Vecchio,[112] the historic covered bridge undamaged by the enemy. At this time I went on a reconnaissance to check out our route of advance, particularly bridge capacity for our 33-ton TDs, and road width through the small villages. Two platoon leaders were in the jeep with me and the driver. The enemy had pulled back and we had lost contact. We found a few bypasses and started back on a different route. We came to a farmhouse with German helmets and weapons at the door. I yelled at the driver to floorboard the jeep; we got our weapons ready and away we went, headed south. Shots rang out from the rear and a haystack on our right partially concealed some lounging Germans. We were shooting and they, surprised, fired as we sped on. Meanwhile, I had to yell at the driver to keep his head up and watch the road. We reached one of our approaching tank columns and Company A TDs less than a half mile from the German positions. I told them to hit every haystack and farmhouse they saw. We were quite excited of course, and even laughed in relief at the close call. We had surprised them and being a speeding target had saved us.

One of the platoon leaders had not fired, sort of frozen through it all. I took him aside and asked him about this. He had no explanation and I saw to it that he was transferred. As a platoon leader in charge of four TDs and 30 men he would have been a disaster. In fact, his platoon sergeant who now took over was recommended for a combat appointment later. A platoon leader must lead; he has daily close contact with his men; he must not fail them. The infantry motto, *Follow Me*, is so appropriate. Resistance was slight north of the Arno for 10 or 15

---

[111] Grassina is a small town near Florence. Today, it is located within Florence's metropolitan area.

[112] The Ponte Vecchio is a medieval stone closed-spandrel segmental arch bridge over the Arno River, in Florence, Italy, noted for still having shops built along it, as was once common. During World War II, the Ponte Vecchio was not destroyed by Germans during their retreat on the advance of the liberating British 8th Army on August 4, 1944, unlike all other bridges in Florence. This was supposedly because of an express order by Hitler himself. However, access to Ponte Vecchio was obstructed by the destruction of the buildings at both ends, which have since been rebuilt using a combination of original and modern design.

miles; then came the German Gothic Line fortifications and the foothills of the Appenines. This was a defensive belt about 60 miles deep consisting of firing trenches, gun pits concrete bunkers, and strong points blocking routes north, situated for mutual fire support. The Futa Pass [113] blocked Highway 65, 20 miles north of Florence and 30 miles south of Bologna and the Po Valley. There was a secondary pass, Il Giogo, 10 miles east of Futa and this would become the main objective of the II Corps—outflanking Futa.

In the II Corps, plan the 91st Division would go for the main objective supported by the 85th Division on the right. This would be east of Highway 65. The 34th Division had a holding mission to the left of the highway and we were attached to them. September 10 was easy going but the 11th brought the first sustained resistance. We had to deploy and find firing positions supporting the lead elements. We could see the Futa Pass a couple of miles to our right. The terrain was hilly, with woods and rocks and few trails. Much foot reconnaissance was needed to find firing positions. At one point, Company C was under fire with lead infantry in a little village overlooking the scene. I left my driver and jeep under cover and started down the trail. Incoming mortar rounds caused me to hit the ground a few times. I got to the village, paused, and then ran down the street toward our guns. I looked for cover in a house to the right with an open door. I dashed in and almost broke my leg on an iron bar that had been thoughtfully left blocking the entrance. I finally got up and went on to contact our people. My leg smarts when I think about it now. War is hell.

The Il Giogo attack was an initial success, and I remember how glad we were to hear of it. A breakthrough in one place generally meant advance on the flanks as the Germans pulled back. In this case, not right away, however. The enemy counterattacked on the 18th and took back some of the ground. You could always count on the counterattack, like the counterpunch in boxing. We continued on the Highway 65 axis against stubborn resistance and in heavy rain, making the trails impassable. The engineers were hard-pressed to keep a minimum road net open, so essential for all vehicles let alone heavy tanks and TDs. On 30 September, the battalion was assigned to the 91st Di-

---

[113] The Futa Pass is a pass in the Tuscan-Emilian Apennines, at an elevation of 903 m (2,963 ft). It is located in the commune of Firenzuola, in the province of Florence. It separated the valleys of Mugello and of the Santerno River. During World War II it was part of the Gothic Line. A German military cemetery was created nearby in the 1950s.

vision, now responsible for the well-defended Highway 65. Radicosa Pass, six miles beyond Futa, was heavily defended and Monghidoro[114] was a key point four miles beyond. The latter was taken on October 4 with our guns contributing both direct and indirect fire. Loiano,[115] another strongpoint, was 3½ miles beyond. A 1000-round artillery preparation—plus air strikes—softened the defenses, but house-to-house fighting ensued and then the inevitable counterattack. We supported from forward positions with direct and indirect fire. Our guns were accurate at 500 to 1000 yards and could respond to infantry requests for pinpoint accuracy. We also fired at suspected enemy observation and strong points on the high ground overlooking the main line of resistance (MLR). Loiano was taken October 5. I would generally be at the supported infantry battalion command post to better understand how we could contribute. This entailed much foot reconnaissance for alternative firing positions. Ammunition supply was a continuing task. We wanted to assure those infantrymen that they were being supported. The sight and sound of those three-inch guns, close at hand, was a great morale builder.

I am reminded now of one of our Company C platoon leaders, Lt. Edgar S. Williamson, son of an Arkansas Baptist Preacher, and therefore called "Deacon." He had gone to Ouachita College,[116] which was noted for its strong ROTC program. Deacon was of slight build, with glasses, appearing more of a school teacher than as a warrior. How deceiving appearances can be; he was utterly fearless under fire. He got through training in good fashion, although I'm sure his platoon wondered how this mild-mannered officer would do. Once committed to action they and we found out. He was invariably at all the hot spots looking for better and closer firing positions. We became good friends. In fact, I loaned him one of my books, Henderson's *Stonewall Jackson*, which we had studied at the Point; another I had with me was a small three-volume *War and Peace*. These books survived the war. I had discussed Stonewall with Deacon and he had borrowed it. Anyways, I came up to his almost inaccessible firing positions near Loiano and his guns were in action firing on a German supply road below. Mortars

---

[114] Monghidoro is a municipality in the Bologna Province in Italy's Emilia-Romagna region. It is approximately 25 miles south of Bologna.

[115] Loiano is also a town in Italy's Bologna Province, located about 22 miles south of Bologna.

[116] Ouachita College is now known as Ouachita Baptist University and is located in Arkadelphia, Arkansas.

had been coming in but I worked my way up to him. He had just been hit in the hand with a fragment and was waiting for medics. He was in tears from the severe pain and said maybe Stonewall would have stayed but he couldn't. A real man; he got the Silver Star for his courage under fire. We were happy to have him back in a few weeks. He has since passed away.

The Livergnano Escarpment [117] was the next objective, about three miles away at an elevation of 1800 feet. It represented the center of the Gothic Line and was well defended. We supported the 91st Division in its attack along Highway 65. Poor visibility and rain limited our air support and observed fire. On October 9 outpost positions were taken, having been pounded with artillery, but the enemy remained—well dug in. His counterattack stopped the attack. A weather break meant air strikes by B-25s and B-26s, 1000 500-lb bombs delivered in four days. On 15 October we were on the objective with the 361st Infantry. The 34th Division relieved the 91st at this time and we remained to support them.

The History of the 91st Division [118] gives an idea of the support given by our battalion. Company A fired 324 direct fire rounds supporting the 361st; they knocked out two mortars, one machine gun, and prompted the surrender of 28 Germans from caves above Livergnano. They said the direct fire from our guns was more than they could take. Company B fired 1296 rounds for the 363rd with "excellent results." The attack continued on the 16th with the 34th to take Mt. Belmonte, two miles northeast of Livergnano and off the highway. The 88th would go for Monte Grande five miles east of Belmonte. The 91st would make a holding attack toward Mt. Adone, about three miles northwest of Livergnano. Our battalion had companies A and B supporting the 91st; Company C was with the 34th, whose 133rd Regiment was to attack Belmonte.

---

[117] The Livergnano Escarpment was a formidable natural barrier located between the Santerno and Po Rivers. At some points the escarpment rose to over 1,800 feet high. At other places, especially toward the upper half of the cliff, it is a perpendicular rock wall. According to a 91st Infantry Division historical record, it was the site of most grinding and heartbreaking fighting the division had ever known.

[118] The *91st Division* history was a 94-page booklet published by the 91st Division during the last months of the war for distribution to the division's soldiers and their families.

The 133rd tried a night attack. Rain, fog and muddy trails made for difficult control. Heavy mortar and artillery fire preceded a German counterattack which stopped the 133rd. The TDs or tanks could not be brought to bear because of the poor going. Meanwhile the 88th and the 85th had success on the right, 22-25 October, causing a German withdrawal from Belmonte. The 91st had gone three miles beyond Livergnano, but Adone still dominated two miles to the west. October 26 brought a strong German counterattack on the right with heavy rains washing out bridges. The II Corps drive for the Po Valley ended here on the northern slopes of the Apennines with Bologna and the Valley eight miles away. It would be spring before the advance continued. Casualties had been higher during these six weeks of fighting than any since the Salerno landings in September 1943. The replacement system was severely strained, all units being understrength and worn out. Artillery ammunition was short and resupply was difficult. Italian service units and pack mules were used to supply mountain locations. The 804th was supporting the 91st Division astride Highway 65 with direct and indirect fire.

Typically, the enemy positions overlooked our lines. Mt. Adone, two miles from the front line, to the northwest, had good observation of Highway 65. Monterumici hill mass was on the front line on the left, with caves and hidden firing positions in the rocky, hilly terrain. On the highway the line was about three miles beyond Livergnano, on a ridge looking down on Pianoro [119] (two miles) and about eight miles from Bologna in the Po Valley. The Fifth Army tactic would include nightly infantry patrols, daily outposts, and air observation all designed to maintain contact. Our battalion had over-watching positions with the infantry as well as artillery positions. Our targets would be known or suspected enemy positions on Monterumici reported by infantry, artillery or our own observers. Nighttime brought our harassing fires, pre-registered during the day and fired on a random schedule during the night. This included our guns and even machine guns. Every infantry patrol was covered by prearranged artillery and mortar fires on call as needed along the patrol route.

---

[119] Pianoro is a town in Italy's Bologna Province in the hills of the Tusco-Emilian Apennines. During World War II, the Pianoro was heavily bombed and was also the site of a fierce battle in October 1944 that destroyed 98.5 percent of the town. The town was later rebuilt two miles north of the original site and called Pianoro Nuovo (New Pianoro).

By this time, the Army was 7000 soldiers understrength in our area and the replacement system had to be built up. There was a shortage of all kinds of ammunition and a limit put on the number of rounds to be fired daily. The enemy kept up sporadic fire on our positions but he had his supply problems as well. The operational slowdown led to a sense of complacency which had to be countered. I inaugurated a training program with one of our platoon leaders in charge. It included refresher (or first time) training in the care and maintenance of field telephone, proper attachment of wires and batteries, and general cleanliness; proper use of range cards, indicating targets, range and azimuth from a given position, to be turned over to the next relieving gun crew; cleanliness of ammunition and radios; and of course TD maintenance. In the heat of an engagement, some of these basic things can get overlooked or taken for granted. I inspected gun positions daily, among other things looking for alternate positions to throw the enemy's range card off. I remember checking one position located in plain view of the skyline with a covered position a few yards away. The crew had not been shot at in days and were now quite careless; it was only a matter of time. I remember telling them that it was not professional. If you are to die for your country, do it in a professional manner. They got off the skyline.

Much needed TD maintenance was performed. Our company and battalion maintenance was outstanding. Our retrievers brought back disabled vehicles from all over the battlefield. We routed platoons (three per company of four TDs each) to the rear so that all got front line relief. It also provided a chance for a five-day R & R (rest and recuperation) in Florence or Rome. R & R: showers, change of clothes, big hotel, good food, drink, singing, dancing and merriment before going back. There were officers' clubs in both cities and we also liberated an apartment in Florence for our own use. The enlisted men had their own facilities. I remember a night club in Rome, big band and beautiful songstress singing *Non Ti Scordar di Me*. I guess I'll always love music. One of our operations sergeants taught me to play chess over these winter months, but I haven't kept up with it. I must learn again. It came in handy during my POW days (April—May 1945).

An illuminating shell had been designed for our three-inch guns and they became very popular in illuminating enemy positions at night. The flare was fired over the target area and the gun or another lowered and fired. We experimented also with air strikes having planes come in precisely on time to drop bombs by the light of the flares. For our night firing missions a target list would come down from division operations with times, location and number of rounds. Sometimes these lists would be slightly altered by the gunners by elevating the gun for a greater range to get those "rear area commandos." Divisions were also given a respite, rotating to reserve and reconstituting. The 88th went in early November, then the 85th and then the 91st. We stayed in place being attached to the relieving units in turn.

The December 16, 1944 German Ardennes offensive [120] had an impact on Italy. Movement of German units toward the Italian west coast was detected and a drive toward Leghorn was feared. The 92nd Division held this sector—an African-American division already tested and found wanting early in October. [121] To be fair, this division had only 25% in mental Category III or above as measured by the Army General Classification Test Score (AGTC); 13% didn't even score, being illiterate. The GTC score was a rough measure of expected performance; a high school graduate in Category II generally outperformed a non-graduate in IV or V in terms of absorbing basic training, discipline and in general adaptability to military life. A report on the subject is found in *The Employment of Negro Troops, US Army in World War II*, Office of the Chief of Military History, US Army, GPO Washington D.C. 1966.

The Selective Service system administered the tests immediately on enlistment. There were five categories depending on scoring:

I   Superior
II   Above Average
III   Average
IV   Below Average
V   Inferior

The Average spread of scores, black and white, in 1942 was:

	White %	Black %
I	6.6	0.4
II	28.0	3.4

---

[120] This was otherwise known to history as the Battle of the Bulge.

[121] Historically, the combat prowess of the 92nd Division has proven to be a controversial subject. While some observers maintained that the quality of soldier was poor in this division, others have attributed the division's lackluster performance to incompetent leadership—particularly that of its commander, Maj. Gen. Edward Almond (1892-1979), and most of his staff.

III	32.1	12.3
IV	24.8	34.7
V	8.5	49.2

The 92nd Division was made up entirely of black enlisted men, with officers of both races. Most of the company grade officers, primarily lieutenants, were black. Obviously, the 92nd had a high percentage of poorly educated men and illiterates. It had been determined that Category I–IIIA (score above 50) enlistees could be expected to perform 10- -20% better than Category IV. In today's volunteer Army the goal is 67% Category I–IIIA; it is actually 70%. Only 2% Category IV are admitted.

The Germans hit the 92nd with a limited objective attack on December 26, 1944. The 366th Regiment fell back in disarray as did the 370th. Two British Indian Brigades and the 1st Armored Division had been moved to block a deep penetration. Our battalion supplied ammunition trucks to help transport the British. They attacked to restore the line finding only a German screening force; they had pulled back after a brief penetration. The 92nd had to be reconstituted before the final Po Valley offensive in April. [122]

---

[122] In fairness, the Medal of Honor was later awarded to two African-American 92nd Division officers in 1997, Lt. John R. Fox (1915-1944)—posthumously—and Lt. Vernon Baker (1919-2010). Lieutenant Fox's Medal of Honor citation reads: *For extraordinary heroism against an armed enemy in the vicinity of Sommocolonia, Italy on 26 December 1944, while serving as a member of Cannon Company, 366th Infantry Regiment, 92d Infantry Division. During the preceding few weeks, Lieutenant Fox served with the 598th Field Artillery Battalion as a forward observer. On Christmas night, enemy soldiers gradually infiltrated the town of Sommocolonia in civilian clothes, and by early morning the town was largely in hostile hands. Commencing with a heavy barrage of enemy artillery at 0400 hours on 26 December 1944, an organized attack by uniformed German units began. Being greatly outnumbered, most of the United States Infantry forces were forced to withdraw from the town, but Lieutenant Fox and some other members of his observer party voluntarily remained on the second floor of a house to direct defensive artillery fire. At 0800 hours, Lieutenant Fox reported that the Germans were in the streets and attacking in strength. He then called for defensive artillery fire to slow the enemy advance. As the Germans continued to press the attack towards the area that Lieutenant Fox occupied, he adjusted the artillery fire closer to his position. Finally he was warned that the next adjustment would bring the deadly artillery right on top of his position. After acknowledging the danger,*

continued...

The winter months saw the supply dumps filling with food, fuel and ammunition. Replacements arrived to fill up the ranks. The 92nd Division made a limited objective attack on our left in the Serchio River valley, [123] 8-11 of February 1945. It failed with no objectives taken. However, to the right of that the newly arrived 10th Mountain Division (27 December) teamed up with the Brazilian Expeditionary Force (BEF) to advance the front line abreast of II Corps, 19 February to 5 March, 1945—just south of Vergato. [124] Advance elements of the BEF had arrived in August 1944, but it wasn't until November that it was up to strength. By March 31 IV Corps had a 50-mile front from the west coast just 15 miles below La Spezia, [125] to the Reno River. [126] The

---

...continued

Lieutenant Fox insisted that the last adjustment be fired as this was the only way to defeat the attacking soldiers. Later, when a counterattack retook the position from the Germans, Lieutenant Fox's body was found with the bodies of approximately 100 German soldiers. Lieutenant Fox's gallant and courageous actions, at the supreme sacrifice of his own life, contributed greatly to delaying the enemy advance until other infantry and artillery units could reorganize to repel the attack. His extraordinary valorous actions were in keeping with the most cherished traditions of military service, and reflect the utmost credit on him, his unit, and the United States Army. Lieutenant Baker's Medal of Honor citation reads: For extraordinary heroism in action on 5 and 6 April 1945, near Viareggio, Italy. Then Second Lieutenant Baker demonstrated outstanding courage and leadership in destroying enemy installations, personnel, and equipment during his company's attack against a strongly entrenched enemy in mountainous terrain. When his company was stopped by the concentration of fire from several machine gun emplacements, he crawled to one position and destroyed it, killing three Germans. Continuing forward, he attacked an enemy observation post and killed two occupants. With the aid of one of his men, Lieutenant Baker attacked two more machine gun nests, killing or wounding the four enemy soldiers occupying these positions. He then covered the evacuation of the wounded personnel of his company by occupying an exposed position and drawing the enemy's fire. On the following night Lieutenant Baker voluntarily led a battalion advance through enemy mine fields and heavy fire toward the division objective. Second Lieutenant Baker's fighting spirit and daring leadership were an inspiration to his men and exemplify the highest traditions of the Armed Forces.

[123] The Serchio River is the third longest river in Italy's Tuscany region.

[124] Vergato is a small municipality in the Province of Bologna located about 25 miles southwest of Bologna.

[125] La Spezia is a port city located midway between Genoa and Pisa on the Ligurian Sea.

NOTHING IMPOSSIBLE

92nd Division had the east (left) sector, with the famous 442nd (Nisei) Regimental Combat Team and the 473rd Regiment (converted air defense artillery units) attached; its 370th Regiment was under division control but the other two (365th, 371st) were under Army control. II Corps had a 22-mile front, from the Reno River east to a point seven miles east of Highway 65; the 1st Armored Division the 85th, and the 88th Divisions were in rear areas training, preparing for the final drive. Our battalion remained supporting the 34th Division in both direct and indirect fire positions.

I generally made the rounds of our positions daily, sharing the chore with the battalion commander. Enemy activity was light with a few mortar and artillery rounds thrown our way daily, enough to make you speed through the observed areas. I remember one day when I was going forward to check a position under enemy observation and fire. A mortar round hit closely and I debated the wisdom of proceeding, from my position on the ground. I had a talk with myself to the effect that West Point did not expect me to cower on the road and then turn back. I told myself to get my butt up, walk leisurely forward to the TD position and to hell with those GD Krauts. So I did, forcing myself to appear nonchalant. Thank the Lord nothing happened.

We worked with many different units and each had its own method of operation. The closer you got to the front the more accurate the information about the situation, particularly as to where the front line was. I would usually check in at division headquarters operations section (G3) to find out which of our units would be supporting what specific regiments. Front line units were indicated on the map. We took this information with a grain of salt. Division always had the line farther forward than was the actual case. The next stop was at regiment to find out what battalions were to be supported. We usually found the regimental commander at a forward command post or with a forward battalion. The next stop was at battalion and here the information became more specific and accurate; the command post would be in a coveted position just behind the rifle companies. But the commander was often at a forward position to be reached with some care. He would point out location of rifle companies and specific targets. Company commanders were invariably delighted at the prospect of three-inch gun support and indicated targets to be fired on. Targets were often

---

...*continued*

[126] The Reno River, located in northern Italy, is the country's tenth longest river.

close and we made careful reconnaissance to pick out the best firing positions. I was usually accompanied by the TD company commander or platoon leader so we had a clear understanding of what was to be done.

I once checked in with one division to ascertain the location of the front line indicated on the map. I then subtracted about a mile from it and went forward. That's where the action actually was. To the grunt on the front line, anything to the rear is the rear echelon; they lead a tough life when in contact with the enemy. Anyways, here is another quick tale about our left flank neighbors, the 92nd Division. They made a preemptive attack on April 5 to seize Massa, [127] a few miles up the coast. The division had been reconstituted to include its original 370th Regiment, the 442nd Regimental Combat team, and the 473rd Regiment (former air defense artillerymen). The division's 365th and 371st Regiments were under Army control (and out of harm's way) to cover the long coastal left flank. The 370th made no progress but the 442d predictably "by nightfall on the 5th...had driven the enemy from several surrounding heights..." and for the next two days pursued the enemy and "...captured Monte Belvedere two miles northeast of Massa."

This gung ho regiment had penetrated 11 miles by 19 April, led most of the way by their famous 100th battalion. The Nisei [128] were drafted from internment camps in California in 1943. They were fiercely proud to be Americans, and they showed it in combat. They took casualties, received many awards, and had no disciplinary problems. Frank Mouri, my daughter Ellen's father-in-law, was in this regiment. He went on to have an outstanding military career; in fact, he was squadron sergeant major of the First Squadron, Fourteenth Cavalry, which I commanded in 1963-1964. Frank says they mounted a banzai charge at one point; I believe him. The 473rd anti-aircraft artillery retreads also did very well, attacking through the 370th positions. This action on the left flank preceded the main event—the breakout into the Po Valley.

---

[127] Massa is a town in Tuscany that is located about three miles from the Tyrrhenian Sea.

[128] Nisei is a Japanese term used in North and South America that denotes children born in the new country to Japanese immigrants.

Chapter 6

POW Days

THE final phase of the Italian Campaign began 15 April 1945 with a tremendous artillery and air preparation. The II Corps on a 15-mile front from left to right had the 6th South African Armored Division, the 88th Division, the 91st Division (on Highway 650), the 34th Division, and the Italian Legnano Battle Group. [129] The South African division was to take Mt. Sole and orient north on Highway 64 into the Po Valley. The 88th Division was to take Monterimici, with its network of strongpoints and caves. Mt. Adone, dominating the area, was the 91st's objective. The 34th Division aimed for high ground to their front, as did the Italians. Our battalion had two companies with the 91st Division's 361st and 363d Regiments and Company C with the 88th's 349th Regiment. I was with Company C and checked in to the battalion headquarters. Our artillery and air bombardment kept the enemy down but when our fire lifted they were back in their positions, aided by minefields and very difficult terrain. The battalion command group, in the basement of a farmhouse, had radio contact with the lead companies and also with regiment. The latter demanded progress but the effort was stopped by minefield and by the difficulty of a night attack. The lead company commander was killed. His replacement was quickly sent down from the battalion staff—a young lieutenant who was killed by a mine an hour later. And still regiment demanded progress. Monterumici was taken the next day, and the 88th began to move to the left to take advantage of the South Africans' progress. By 19 April we were moving into high ground overlooking the valley. Pockets of resistance remained but the Po Valley could be seen in the distance.

---

[129] The Italian Legnano Battle Group was likely a formation of the Italian Co-Belligerent Army, which was the name applied to the Royal Italian Army when if fought on the side of the Allies from 1943 onwards during World War II.

This next section deals with the breakthrough and my subsequent capture. The U.S. Fifth Army broke out of its winter positions in the Appenines, south of Bologna during the period 14–20 April 1945. The 804th Tank Destroyer Battalion, I as the executive officer, was attached to the 88th Division, just west of Highway 64, which led into the city. On April 19, we were in position overlooking the Po Valley, held up by stubborn resistance offered by the German 8th Mountain Division. I, then a major, was with a task force which included tank destroyers, tanks, and infantry. We were moving along a ridge under enemy artillery, mortar, and small arms fire. We were all exhausted from the last few days of combat. The infantry particularly were trying to regroup. An enemy strongpoint in a farmhouse up ahead was holding us up. I went up to find out what was going on and could find no one in charge. I went back to the leading infantry and tank platoon commanders and outlined a plan. Very simply, we would lead with the tanks in column and deploy to attack the farmhouse, while the infantry proceeded up a draw to take the position from the rear. After neutralizing the position we would split into two columns and advance on two roads down into the Po Valley.

I climbed onto the back deck of the lead tank, armed with my pistol, and we moved out. Although exposed, I had good visibility and could direct fire at the house from which small arms fire was coming. A couple of tank rounds stopped the German firing. A platoon of infantry circled around to the right and we kept moving. A wounded German crawled by with one hand upraised, saying "kamerad." I almost shot him, thinking he was going to throw a grenade, but then motioned him on to the rear. Having secured the position we moved out according to plan, entering the Po Valley just west of Bologna. What a welcome sight it was after those months in the mountains, so limiting to mobile armor operations. I received the Distinguished Service Cross for this action. [130]

I stayed with this task force as it proceeded north, with the infantry riding tanks and tank destroyers. I had my jeep, driven by Roy Johnson—a very fine soldier. Sometime on April 19, I got a radio message to rejoin the battalion with the 804th elements. The battalion was being attached to the 91st Division a few miles to the east. Since we had one platoon of tank destroyers already well ahead with a task force, I told the company commander (Joe Clark, Company C) to pro-

---

[130] Refer to the Appendix C for the Distinguished Service Cross Citation.

ceed as ordered and that I would get word to lead the platoon. Johnson and I continued north following tank tread and other signs of the task force well ahead of us. As we approached a small village the road and tacks veered to the left. I told Johnson to drive into the village and to see if there were any signs of activity. As we approached we saw the villagers waving from windows and calling out. We continued for about 300 yards and then I told Johnson to turn around and head back. Just then two armed Germans jumped up ahead of us and ran across the road; we had apparently flushed them out, so others had to be around. Johnson turned the jeep, I pulled my pistol, and we started back.

Small arms fire broke out immediately from the shoulder of the road on our right. We had been ambushed. I'm sure the villagers had not realized the Germans were so close or they would have hidden out. Anyway, I remember trying to fire my pistol and then realizing the safety was on. At the same time, I noticed that the jeep was slowing down and veering to the left. I turned to tell Johnson to keep his eye on the road and speed up, but he wasn't there. He had been shot out of the jeep and killed as it turned out. I reached across to take the wheel and tried to get back on the road, but it was too late. The vehicle went into the shoulder and flipped onto its side. My head hit the steering wheel and stunned me for a few seconds.

Firing continued in my direction and then stopped when a German captain appeared, aimed a pistol at me, and told me in English to put my hands up. From the amount of shooting that had transpired they must have thought I had a squad with me. I got onto my feet with my hands up and my captor motioned me to start down the road away from the village. I asked him about my driver and he said that he had been killed.

Poor Johnson had apparently been hit by the first burst of fire, which had gone right past my head. I had been very lucky. Roy was a fine soldier and an excellent driver. [131] We had been through a lot together. I later wrote to his mother in Bruno, Minnesota. She wrote back thanking me for writing, and saying that she knew her son died doing his duty for his country. It was a touching letter. I'm sorry that I have since lost it.

---

[131] Pvt. Roy M. Johnson was later buried in the American Cemetery in Florence, Italy. He resides in Plot H, Row 10, Grave 5. Among his decorations were the Purple Heart, the American Campaign Medal, and the World War II Victory Medal.

I went down the road with my hands locked behind my head—the captain following with his pistol drawn. We had indeed ridden into an ambush. I passed several riflemen and a machine gun or two, the men all laughing and pointing at me. Then about 100 yards farther I saw a towed antitank gun, camouflaged, and directed down the road toward the village. Obviously we had been headed right for the position. The crew was particularly amused, making gestures of pulling the lanyard. My captor left me with a battalion headquarters group in a small farmhouse. They sat me down, gave me some water, but did no interrogating. In a while, near dusk, a few soldiers on bicycles arrived to take me back to the rear. I was provided with a bicycle and we left. After travelling for a mile or so we stopped at a villa which I believe was a regimental command post. It was now after dusk.

Another group took charge and I was taken inside to a room appointed like a den or a library. A colonel was seated at a desk with a lieutenant interpreter at his side. A couple of guards placed themselves behind me. I stood at attention and saluted. The colonel was smoking and he offered me a cigarette, which I declined. He asked me what unit I was from and what our plans were. I remember thinking that the moment of truth was at hand. Anyway, I told him my name, rank and serial number, and also that by the rules of the Geneva Convention that was all I should divulge. I remember that he looked at me, talked to the lieutenant, and then said that they had my jeep and belongings; of course the bumper markings identified the unit. That ended the interrogation and I was escorted out into the courtyard. It was now dark and flashes of artillery fire lit up the landscape. Our artillery was harassing the general area and a few rounds came rather close. My captors huddled under cover but kept me in the open on the ground. Undoubtedly they felt that it would be poetic justice if I were hit by my own artillery.

An hour or so later there was much commotion and movement, and a horse drawn column formed on the road. I was put in the wagon, seated at the driver's feet, facing him and his assistant. My back was to a pair of horses, my hands behind my head but not tied. There were five or six Germans in the back of the wagon. The column started north on a dusty backcountry road. I had a good appreciation of how well the Germans employed camouflage, borne out by how well the column had been hidden during the day when our Air Force had been out in strength. Haystacks, barns, woods, houses were all used for concealment; strict discipline was enforced. At night all secondary roads were jammed with units withdrawing to the north, with selected units detailed to fight a delaying action covering the withdrawal. Meanwhile, a mile or so to the west our tanks were speeding toward the Po River on an undefended main road.

We went on for a couple of hours and then small arms fire was heard up ahead and off to the flanks. Italian partisans had now become a factor and they were attacking the column. We halted in the dark and troops were developed to counter the threat. At this time one of my captors, a sergeant who had once lived in Brooklyn, warned me in English not to try and escape, that the war was over for me. Actually, this was probably the best chance to escape that I had as a prisoner. It was dark and there was much confusion and running around. I lay still in the darkness and briefly thought of quickly jumping and running away. Chances of meeting stray Germans were high, however, and a new group might not want to take prisoners. In any event, I kept still and at the all clear signal we all got back into the wagon.

At dawn we reached a temporary assembly area and quickly dispersed in small groups to continue the trek north. The sergeant was in charge of me, in a group of about eight other Germans. I saw no other prisoners until I was interned days later in Bolzano. [132] We proceeded toward the Po on foot, avoiding main roads and staying in the shadow of tree lines where possible.

The weather was fine and our planes were over continuously, looking for targets including the Po River bridges farther to the north. The Germans were adept at using all forms of concealment while at the same time continuing to move. If caught in the open with a plane in a position to observe we became motionless, hoping to escape detection. When the plane banked away we quickly began moving again. Anyone who spotted a plane in a position to observe would shout "flierger" and we would freeze. I became a pretty good spotter myself, not wishing to become an Air Force statistic at this late stage. I remember one day as we were riskily crossing a field in the open, a soldier on horseback, camouflaged with branches and bush trotted by. A plane appeared in the distance and we all stopped, including the horseman. It was remarkable to see that horse remain motionless, as if he realized that lives depended on his not moving. We escaped detection and continued on.

---

[132] Bolzano is the capital of the South Tyrol Province in northern Italy and is the largest city in the area. Today, it is home to the Italian Army's Alpini High Command (COMALP).

We arrived at the Po in the vicinity of Ostiglia [133] a few days after I was captured. There were no bridges intact and in fact an ammunition dump had been nearby, sending exploding shells intermittently our way. We prepared to swim the Po, timing our start with the finish of an air strike, hoping to cross before the next one. We stripped down to our shorts and piled our gear onto a makeshift raft before plunging into the river. I took a position at the front, swimming with one hand and pulling with the other. The rest of the group took positions around the raft and we slowly made progress across as well as downstream. We kept on the alert for planes and finally got across safely. On the far side we ran for cover, dressed, and hurried on.

We were heading for Verona [134] and the Adige River, [135] about 25 miles away. Our days followed a pattern of walking, avoiding detection, and resting at isolated farmhouses at night. Rations were slim, and when we reached a stopping place for the night a foraging party was sent out by the person in charge, while the rest of us dozed and waited, seated or sprawled on the floor. A typical meal for the group would be a couple of chickens, perhaps a few eggs, a little baloney, bread, lard, and perhaps some wine. It was never very much, and generally there were perhaps a dozen or so of us. The officer or noncom in charge would divide the spoils equitably, including a share for me, and then we would eat. Guards were posted while we slept. Just before dawn we were up and on our way. The makeup of the group seemed to change daily except for the sergeant who had been originally charged with my keep.

I was struck by the discipline still evident among the Germans. The ranking noncommissioned or commissioned officer was definitely in charge. I remember one night when we reached a farmhouse after a harrowing day. Exhausted, we stretched out around the bare living room. A young second lieutenant was in charge. Suddenly a paratrooper came storming into the room, excited and talking loudly. He spotted the lieutenant, came to attention, saluted and apologized for his outburst. He was motioned to a corner. Then the foraging party

---

[133] Ostiglia is a municipality in the Province of Mantua in Italy's Lombardy region. It is located about 100 miles southeast of Milan.

[134] Verona is a city straddling the Adige River in Veneto, northern Italy. Today, it is one of the main tourist destinations in northern Italy.

[135] The Adige River is the second longest river in Italy at 250 miles in length (The Po River, at 405 miles, is the longest). Its source is in the South Tyrol Province near Austria and Switzerland.

arrived, the rations allotted, and we ate with little talk. On another occasion we approached a deep swift-running stream about 50 yards wide. I was with the first group to arrive, and there was much milling about. A small boat was found with room for eight. Discussion ensued about the order of crossing, with a great sense of urgency since we were prime targets for an air attack. A major arrived with a party of three. He immediately barked out commands which sent all hands to the cover of a nearby farmhouse to await further orders. He detailed two men to look for ropes and paddles. These were found and he then appointed the first group to cross. Meanwhile, the ropes had been attached to the front and rear of the boat. Two men on the rear bank played out the rope as the boat was paddled across with its first load. On the far bank, two men were similarly detailed to handle the rope while a detail of two paddled back. The hasty improvisation and organization of effort brought order out of confusion and the crossing went smoothly.

The next major crossing was over the Adige River, in the general vicinity of Legnago. [136] We were under intermittent air attack throughout another beautiful April day. I could see the bridge we were headed for to our front. It had already been struck several times and was a mass of twisted girders. Wooden planks afforded a precarious path through the girders, the river being some distance below. We crouched in brush near the river bank waiting for the best time to make a try. A pair of P-47 attack aircraft strafed the bridge heading straight for us, spraying .50 caliber bullets in the vicinity. They hadn't seen us however and we remained crouched, timing the period between the attacks. It was tense. The planes had been successful in catching a few bridge crossers before we had arrived. This was attested to by a very excited paratrooper sergeant who suddenly joined our group. He began to shout, pointing at me and taking out his pistol. My captor, the sergeant, told me to remain quiet and not to move. Apparently the soldier had a few friends caught on the bridge earlier and was intent on evening the score. Reason prevailed and he finally left. Meanwhile, it was decided to make a break for the bridge. We ran, jumped on the nearest plank, and started across, holding onto the girders and balancing precariously on the planks. The crossing took only a few minutes but it seemed like all afternoon. We made it safely and ran quickly away after reaching the other side. Our next assembly area was to be

---

[136] Legnago is a small town in the Province of Verona in northern Italy. Traces of human presence in the area date back to the Bronze Age.

Trento,[137] about 40 miles to the north on Highway 12, running north-south in a narrow valley; a pass through the Dolomites[138] and the Alps.

I was treated quite well throughout the whole period. For example, I had an equal share of food and complete freedom of movement, under guard of course. When we talked it was mostly about personal matters—home, family, and the like. We spoke broken English or broken German to make ourselves understood; of course my captor spoke English pretty well. They knew that the war would soon be over for them, as it was now for me. I remember at the close of one long grueling day we came to a large farmhouse, almost a villa. Several groups began to gather, and there were 40 or 50 of us finally, I being the only prisoner. A major took charge, sent out foragers, and had the rest of us sit alongside the house in the shadows. A few Italian retainers had remained and they produced food and wine. When all was ready we were called inside to what in effect had become a banquet hall. The living and dining rooms had been so arranged, with sheets used as table cloths and flowers and candles on each table. I was given a seat next to the major at the head of the table. Wine was passed around and several roast chickens were divided among us, together with salami, bread and lard, used as butter. I could not eat the lard but they seemed to like it. In fact, my captor supposedly did me a favor by offering me an extra lard sandwich. There was much talk, toasts, and even some singing. The major talked at length about his career in a mixture of German and English. I talked about myself as well. We stayed away from military topics.

After the banquet and the wine, we arranged the room for sleeping. Two mattresses were produced, the major having one and I the other, at his insistence. I guess he felt RHIP[139] even with his prisoners. I still remember the whole scene vividly—the beautiful spring evening, the villa, banquet arrangement, and the escape from reality for a few hours. From Legnago we hitched a bus ride to Verona, about 25 miles away. I attracted little attention; although I'm sure we got on the bus

---

[137] Trento is located in the Adige River Valley in Trentino-Alto Adige/Südtirol, an autonomous region in northern Italy. Formerly part of Austria, it was annexed by Italy in 1919.

[138] The Dolomites are a mountain range located in northeastern Italy. The Dolomites are nearly equally shared between the provinces of Belluno, South Tyrol and Trentino

[139] RHIP is an acronym for "rank has its privileges."

because of my prisoner status. I was wearing my khaki shirt, trousers, boots, no helmet, and had a thin German blanket slung over my shoulder. My watch and West Point class ring had been taken from me initially but were returned a few days later.

We got to Verona without incident on or about 25 April. My captor tried to turn me over to a major headquarters without success. Being a ground forces officer, I was headed elsewhere. Disappointing news since it meant taking the road again. I discussed the matter with my captor and suggested that next time I present my case. He seemed to agree. From Verona we bussed north to Trento, 40 miles away and just getting into the Alps. Again no luck with interment and we went on to Bolzano, another assembly area and a major headquarters (Army Group C, SS General Karl Wolff). [140] The city was very active with not much sign of destruction. An amusing incident occurred here. The German Red Cross had organized a soup kitchen in a large hall—wooden benches and tables and steaming containers of soup with black bread on the side. It smelled delicious. My group of eight wanted to downplay the fact that I was a prisoner since it might attract too much attention. I was to pretend that I was a Czech since apparently they wore khaki also, and I could avoid talking. We went through the line and began to eat. We were very hungry and the food was wonderful. A couple of soldiers sat down near me and immediately began asking questions. My captor explained that I was a Czech and didn't speak any German. My interrogator laughed and said that he spoke Czech. I couldn't help laughing at the situation and explained in very halting German that I was a "gefangenen" and an "Amerikkanischen." The word got around quickly and there was a lot of laughing and gesturing. In fact they made sure that I got seconds.

Later that day—28 April 1945—we reported to a German headquarters in the city and I was finally admitted to a makeshift POW prison located in a former schoolhouse. I joined 20 U.S. Air Force prisoners—members of bomber crews shot down over the Brenner Pass. [141] There were four or five officers including a captain. I was the

---

[140] Karl Wolff (1900-1984) was a general of the Waffen-SS. He served as chief of personal staff to Heinrich Himmler and as SS liaison officer to Hitler until 1943. He ended World War II as supreme commander of all SS forces in Italy.

[141] The Brenner Pass is one of the principal passes of the range in the Alps along the border of Italy and Austria. It has therefore been highly coveted throughout history.

ranking officer and therefore in charge of the group. We slept on wooden double bunks with a woolen blanket for cover. We were fed soup and two thin slices of black bread twice a day. Exercise consisted of a walk in the schoolyard for about an hour each morning. We were left quite to ourselves. We improvised a makeshift chess set from scraps of lumber and in fact started a tournament. We also played games like "Ghost" in which we sat in a circle and in turn added letters to words in such a way that hopefully the word would not end at your turn. Taking naps was also a favorite pastime. Rumors of partisan activity in the area were whispered to us by the Italian cooks as we filed past for rations, always with the prospect of imminent freedom. But we were much too realistic to believe any of these.

I was sort of a novelty among my group being a ground force officer. My companions were accustomed to life at an air base with few restrictions. A few of them took to joking with the guard, a not very swift party, and in fact began to call him "apfelkopf" (applehead) and other such names. I finally had a meeting and pointed out that we should maintain some semblance of discipline or we might get our food cut off for a day or two. In other words don't fool with the Germans. We soon began to get whispers that our troops were getting closer. Hard to believe but on May 2 the commandant, a major, came to the door and asked for me, saying that an armistice had been signed. I told him to stop kidding but he insisted and asked me to come to his office. There he told me that the forces in Italy had surrendered but that word had not reached all units. Some fighting was still going on, and it would be best if we stayed together until our forces came north. We were to be released from guard and moved across town to the airfield with his guard detail. He asked me what I wanted in particular and thus I got a tooth brush. He then really surprised me by giving me an Italian Beretta pistol with ammunition just in case I might need it.

Once at the airfield we had only to wait for our forces coming north. We put out strips of cloth forming the letters POW, hoping that a plane might see it and report. The wait seemed interminable although actually only a couple of days. We posted a man on the highway to flag down the first U.S. vehicle. The major and his guard were still with us. Finally, on May 5 a 10th Mountain Division ammunition truck was diverted after several vehicles sped by seeming to ignore us. We scrambled aboard and then I told them to wait. Somehow I felt it only right to take our leave of our captors, who were soon to be prisoners themselves. I ran to the operations center and left a note for the major: Good bye, good luck, we're on our way.

The convoy was headed for the Swiss border and it was quite cold. We reached our destination at dark and then were treated royally to a big meal. As I remember it was pancakes, c-rations, coffee, plus a change of clothes and pup tents. I had to conduct a class for my Air Force colleagues on erecting pup tents and using latrines. Blankets were issued and we were quite comfortable. We spent two nights with these most hospitable artillerymen, and then caught a ride on their re-supply trucks headed for Fifth Army Headquarters at Verona. Of course we had made sure that word of our release had been sent back, knowing that the folks at home would want to know soonest—in my case Mother and Dad. [142]

I guess I could have been processed for a stateside trip right then along with the others. But I had been too long with the 804th for that. I saw Brig. Gen. Guy O. Kurtz, [143] Army Artillery Officer, whom I had met when we supported the 88th Division a few months earlier. He arranged a flight—a two-seated artillery liaison plane—to Feltre [144] where my battalion was now located. What a reunion we had, 7 May 1945. Apparently, a Fifth Army detachment passing through Bolzano had liberated a large stock of champagne and cognac. Each unit received a share, and a very enlightened member of our staff knew about mixing French 75's—a combination of both. What a party and what a headache. A week or so later Fred Rowell, Battalion Commander, and a good one was on orders to return to the States. I became CO on June 4, 1945. We were now at Montecarini near Leghorn, awaiting shipment home. With a new contingent of personnel we were headed for Japan. So green was the unit that I felt it necessary to put out a very basic instruction on section leader duties.

The veterans were leaving daily and I had new men and officers when we boarded our Victory ship, the *Marine Raven*, [145] on 18 July. We landed at Newport News, Virginia on 31 July. A welcoming band

---

[142] Refer to Appendix E for the telegram to the Clements about the MIA status.

[143] Brig. Gen. Guy O. Kurtz was a Pennsylvania native who served as division artillery commander for the 88th Infantry Division. He was later in charge of all artillery for the Fifth Army.

[144] Feltre is a small town in the Belluno Province in northern Italy. The Dolomites loom to the north of the town.

[145] The SS *Marine Raven* was a Type C4-class ship, the largest cargo ships built by the United States Maritime Commission (MARCOM) during World War II.

had met us, a big steak dinner, and we were quickly processed for 30 days leave. We were to reassemble at Fort Hood for training prior to shipment to Japan. The bombs were dropped while we were on leave and orders for inactivation met us when we regrouped in Texas. I was reassigned to Fourth Army Headquarters, Fort Sam Houston, San Antonio, 11 October 1945. After a brief stay here I volunteered to go back to Germany for occupation duty—but that's another story.

Chapter 7

Lessons Learned from World War II

MY subject here is one that is very easy to reflect upon. For those of us who served, the World War II years left their mark on us all. Our experiences taught us many things. Some of these things we have absorbed unconsciously, to be drawn on later. Others are quite vivid in our minds. I have selected three of the latter variety as my contribution. The three are, first—doing the impossible, second—being ready for the unexpected, and third—watching for weakness in subordinates during times of stress. To properly set the stage, let me say that I was a member of a tank destroyer battalion throughout the war, serving successively as company commander, battalion executive officer, and finally battalion commander. The battalion went overseas in August 1942, returned to the U.S. for a brief respite in 1943, and finally returned for deactivation in July 1945. During this period we were in England, Ireland, Africa, and Italy. It was in Italy that we saw all of our combat—from the Garigliano River [146] in March 1944 to the finish in the Alps in May 1945.

It seems to me now that no one had ever told us in training that there is virtually nothing "impossible" in war. The idea of "doing the impossible" has been mentioned in a book on Stonewall Jackson: [147]

> The exertions that he demanded of them seemed beyond the powers of mortal men, but with Jackson leading them the troops felt themselves able to accomplish impossibilities. "I never saw one of Jackson's couriers approaching," said Ewell, "without expecting an order to assault the North Pole!" But

---

[146] The Garigliano River is located in central Italy and is approximately 25 miles in length.

[147] Subsequent research has not been able to identify the exact book from which this statement and quote emerged.

had the order been given neither Ewell nor the Valley troops would have questioned it.

The subject of the impossible doesn't come in any eight or thirteen week training program—sandwiched in with gas mask drill, scouting and patrolling, and like subjects. Somewhere along the line we learned it, though. I know that we all saw situations crop up which apparently offered no solution—everyone shaking their head and making dire predictions.

Then somehow or other a plan was made and the solution finally came about. Take, for example, the time of the tank alert in April 1944. Our battalion was attached to an infantry division, with A and C companies in indirect fire positions, and B company in covered direct fire positions. It was late in the afternoon when word came down to A and C companies of an impending enemy armored attack. The division was quite perturbed, to put it mildly. How long would it take to get out of position and assemble about one half mile from there? Headquarters wanted to know. The answer came back—one half an hour—and so it was. In half an hour the companies were on the road, ammunition loads had been adjusted for direct fire, and the march started. Night had fallen—roads were not entirely discernible or well known—and the mission was to move up to reinforce B company's positions, ready to withstand the enemy armor.

Well, the march was made, positions were picked by guess and by God, and at daybreak the battalion was ready. Of course we bunched up slightly, and the position was not the best imaginable, but all in all for a night march, reconnaissance, selection, and occupation, they were not so bad. One company commander had been very agitated throughout this operation. Night marches on strange ground, facing an unknown threat, were a little too much—well nigh impossible according to him. In fact while the deed was being accomplished he refused to believe that it could be done. Impossible? No—just a little bit different. Certainly we took chances—but after all, we were getting paid for that. As an anticlimax, the enemy armored attack didn't materialize. The report had been false. A cub pilot had thought he had sighted enemy tanks, etc. Well, two company commanders learned something that night—the other never did. The incident was merely a starter on this "impossible" business.

Another event stands out in my mind. We had just entered Rome with one of the leading divisions. Fighting had been bitter on the outskirts, but it looked as if the Krauts had finally pulled back through the city. Our mission was to be on the other side of the city at the banks of the Tiber River [148] at dawn, in order to support further advance of the division. It seemed to be a simple enough thing to do, until you weighed the fact that the city was a maze of blacked-out streets, with crowds of civilians to add to the confusion. About midnight, the following report came back from one of our companies: "Impossible to get to the river—company split up too badly—too dark for further movement—will assemble on the south side of the city and move at daylight." The reaction at battalion headquarters of course was "nuts," or something more explicit. A staff officer went out, got the company collected, and led them through the city to the appointed place. Another "impossible" mission had been cleared up, this one not so difficult. Incidentally, there was a new company commander the next day.

I remember another incident. This time the mission was to put direct fire on a little town in order to neutralize and harass the enemy there. From a study of the map and terrain—it seemed to be impossible to do. The terrain was hilly and cut up, and the town was nestled in a little ravine. We didn't sell short our company commander, Arkansas native Lt. Edgar S. Williamson, though. [149] As mentioned earlier in this book, this boy, known to us as "Deacon," had been superior all the way through. If he said "no," then the answer was probably "no." But he didn't. He studied his map, found one possibility that the average man wouldn't have seen, or wouldn't have wanted to see, and moved into the only spot from which the mission could be accomplished. True, the position was exposed, and a lot of fire came back, but the job was done. We lost one of our best when Lieutenant Williamson was wounded a few days later. These various situations, plus many others, taught me clearly that if the first reaction to a mission is "impossible," then an attempt is being made to get out of it. The impossibility usually exists only in the mind, and the determined soldier usually will find a way.

Another lesson learned has been that of the unexpected and unusual being the normal situation. In other words, no matter how carefully we plan, something always seems to happen to throw the plan out of gear. I believe most of us have learned this fact through experience by now, but the men we may train in the future haven't learned this yet.

---

[148] The Tiber River is the third longest river in Italy at approximately 252 miles in length.

[149] First Lieutenant Edgar S. Williamson was a recipient of the Silver Star as well as the Purple Heart.

They don't even suspect it. Commandos and Rangers will train for this. The following is a quote from a pamphlet on British commandos: "The idea that no type of operation is unusual is inculcated in the men. At a moment's notice they should be able to ride bicycles or motorcycles; Drive automobiles and trucks of unfamiliar types, etc."

So also, from a pamphlet on Japanese parachute troops: "Japanese parachute troops must be thoroughly trained to adapt themselves to any unforeseen situation. They must be trained to fight with limited equipment, etc." I believe that something on this order should be included in all problems, and even everyday routine. How else can we be realistic, and develop flexibility, resourcefulness, and confidence in being able to handle any situation?

I have seen this "unusual" routine demonstrated many times before, during, and after combat, and shall continue to do so undoubtedly in the future. Take for example, that period in our training where we learned artillery methods. We were in Africa training with an infantry division at the time. Orders came down of a new concept for the tank destroyers, i.e., we would learn to fire as artillery, using artillery fire control instruments. Well, the elaborate training program which was in progress was rapidly junked. Division artillery sent over a cadre, and in three weeks we were firing indirect fire and using our equipment properly. Some old artillerymen in the outfit were amazed that it could be done in such a short time. Of course we had this in our favor—the men liked it, and anything they liked they learned to do quickly. Here then was the situation where the training doctrine of the tank destroyers was changed abruptly. Two missions were now envisaged—both direct and indirect fire.

Also, I'll never forget the time we were given another distasteful job, but yet one that gave us valuable experience—and quite unusual experience, too. The African campaign had just ended and our battalion was located in a training area south of Oran, Algeria. Overnight we were given the mission of escorting German POWs back to England. Well, we had not trained for escort guard duty, nor did we look forward to it, naturally. However, one week later, we were on the high seas, performing our duty acceptably, thoroughly familiar with the new routine. After overcoming our initial distaste for the job, the rest had become easy. Plans had been made hurriedly but carefully, and the rest had taken care of itself.

Of course some of the most trying situations were those which confronted a company commander or platoon leader during an attack, when the terrain suddenly showed up different from the map, and hurried change in plans had to be made. Our reconnaissance company pushed out toward the town of Castiglioncello, [150] Italy, one day, with the mission of seizing the town and the high ground beyond. Opposition was slight and progress was rapid until the town was reached. Here a blown bridge was found, with no other way to get into town, at first glance. The company commander was not to be stopped, however. He found a stairway leading down to an escarpment along the bay, and then another stairway leading up into the town—similar to those on the Seine River. [151] Well, that was the answer, and the company was on its objective in an hour, surprising the Krauts on the hill no end. Resourcefulness had paid off.

And so I have come to know that being flexible and resourceful in the face of the unexpected brings confidence, and pays big dividends. I believe this point should be stressed in our training. All should be trained to meet the unexpected—to realize that in combat, situations are not clear cut, with only one or two logical solutions, but rather are usually hazy. Opportunities for decisive results must be grasped as they come. You've got to be flexible, to be able to change your plan quickly as the situation develops; and resourceful, to be able to create a favorable situation where originally one may not have existed.

Another important lesson was that of learning to judge men quickly and accurately under fire. Combat presents many tests, and by them it either develops soldiers, or shows up those who are not. I don't know exactly how these tests can be duplicated in training; they probably cannot. In any event, some weaknesses can be caught in training. Latent weakness will come out in combat. Originally it may be hard to find, but if there, it will finally blossom. Lt. A is a case in point. He went on a reconnaissance with two other officers one day. Part of the journey was covered by jeep, but the remainder, near the front line, on foot. On dismounting Lt. A at once volunteered to stay with the jeep—guarding it, presumably. This was the first indication of weakness on his part. The other two officers went on and returned after completing their job. On the return trip the party ran through a German ambush; a few shots were exchanged but no damage done. This really shook Lt. A. The other two, after getting through safely, laughed and joked about it—a more or less natural way to let off your pent up emotion. Lt. A said not a word. The next day he went to the hospital with some obscure disorder, and he was eventually transferred from the unit

---

[150] Castiglioncello is a renowned sea resort located in Tuscany.
[151] The Seine River is a 483 mile-long river located in France's Paris Basin.

without ever returning. Here, two relatively minor points had betrayed the man, i.e., his staying with the jeep, and his inability to shake off the effects of his close call.

Another man, Lt. B, fooled us for a while. He took his platoon on a mounted patrol (armored cars and jeeps) one afternoon and came back dismounted with one-half of his men a few hours later. His story was that they had been surprised by an ambush and were lucky to get away. How many had been hit, we asked. He didn't know. Where were the others? All had scattered. They finally straggled back. After a day or two we advanced again and recovered the vehicles, unscathed. We were unable to get a clear picture of what had happened from anyone involved, and so tucked the incident away for future reference. A few days later, Lt. B was to take his platoon, this time dismounted, and support an armored car attack on a few enemy held houses. The objective was reached by the mounted element. The dismounted men were due at any time to mop up. They didn't arrive, and finally word came by radio for the vehicles to return. Upon reorganizing it was found that Lt. B had progressed about fifty yards when he and his platoon had been "pinned down" by small arms fire. No one had been hurt, and no one had done any firing back at the enemy. Well, that ended Lt. B with us. We knew that men will go anywhere if properly led, but without proper leadership they normally won't move.

The only unfortunate part of the whole affair was that Lt. B was transferred to a back section unit where he wouldn't have to worry about the enemy. Reclassification was difficult and time consuming, and we were in too much of a hurry to waste further effort on the fellow. I believe that this situation, whereby those failing at the front were sent to unite in the rear, has been recognized by the War Department as one needing correction. Now, I believe, there is some provision being made by which an officer must be reduced to the ranks and kept at the front in the event of showing the "white feather," a much more logical solution.

Lieutenants A and B were only two. There were others, as there were in all units. The commander must be alert to read these men correctly and quickly in order to save lives, and accomplish his mission. And these men are not easy to distinguish. Little things usually happen first to give a warning, and there are signs that should be caught. All of these men like Lt. A and Lt. B usually had two common distinguishing traits. First, it seemed that they were always being given the "impossible" missions, and second, they always had an alibi for failure. Lt. C was particularly good at the latter. He supposedly couldn't fire his platoon from their new positions because they were too exposed; and yet a platoon fifteen hundred yards to his flank in equally exposed position, closer to the front, had been firing for several weeks. That was Lt. C's give-away, and he soon failed completely later on. Don't get the impression that our unit was exemplified by Lieutenants A, B, and C. These are the isolated examples from which we all learned. We did our job as well as the next and took proper satisfaction and pride in accomplishing our missions. Our reputation was good. I've rambled on in the past few pages over a few of the things I learned which I did not find in books or manuals. I believe that others who have been in combat have learned from them too. Certainly they are worth spending some time on in training. All should learn that they can do the impossible; that the unexpected must be looked for and turned to advantage; and that subordinate leaders must be studied closely in training, and tested as much as possible in order to get to their true nature.

Anyways, back to my own story. Following my post-World War II stateside service, I served on occupation duty in Germany, commanding the 17th Mechanized Cavalry Reconnaissance Squadron from 1946 to 1947. In 1948, I took the Armor Advanced Course at Fort Knox, Kentucky and then had a tour with the Training Literature Department of the School, serving in that capacity until 1951. While stationed at Knox I also met and married Martha Mansfield in 1951. An earlier marriage in 1942, just before shipping out, ended in divorce in 1943 while I was serving in North Africa. [152] It was a typical wartime romance complete with "Dear John" letter. I concluded this brief peacetime respite by attending the Command and General Staff College in 1952. However, after that the Korean War beckoned and I was off to fight in another conflict.

---

[152] The name of Mr. Clement's first wife was Jane, and she went on to marry a U.S. Air Force officer. Her last communication with Mr. Clement was in 1966, when she called him to offer her congratulations on his promotion to brigadier general.

Epilogue

ON September 20, 1952 we boarded trains at Pusan for the trip to Inchon on the west coast, the port famous for MacArthur's famous 1950 landing. We clutched our precious personnel records and tried to make ourselves comfortable on straight-backed wooden seats. As we were about to leave, a gang of young urchins [153] appeared armed with rocks. We hit the floor as the rock barrage took its toll of windows, and we pulled slowly out of the yard. Welcome to Korea. We arrived in Inchon after an all-night trip and found division trucks ready to pick us up. I can still recall the stench of the first village we came to—Yong Dong Po. [154] It was hot and the smell of the fertilizer—human excrement, called night soil—plus the open sewage almost made me sick. In about five hours we reached the division rear area. An officer met and welcomed me (I was by this time a lieutenant colonel), assigned me to an officer's tent and told me I would be dining at the General's Mess for dinner. [155] There were drinks before dinner and I got to meet the staff, a very cordial group.

I sat at the division commander's table with him and his assistant commander. I had met them on my trip several days before—Maj. Gen. David L. Ruffner [156] and Brig. Gen. P. D. Ginder. [157] Ruffner had

---

[153] An urchin is defined as a mischievous young child, especially one who is poorly or raggedly dressed.

[154] Yong Dong Po is located on the western outskirts of Seoul.

[155] Mr. Clement was reporting for duty as commander of the 245th tank battalion, 45th Infantry Division.

[156] David L. Ruffner (1896-1973) was a West Virginia native who graduated from Virginia Military Institute in 1917. He served in the U.S. Army from 1917 to 1953 and retired at the rank of major general.

[157] Philip De Witt Ginder (1905-1968) was a New Jersey native who graduated from West Point in 1927. He served in the U.S. Army from 1927 to 1963

continued...

been an artilleryman with the 10th Mountain Division in Italy in World War II. He was a hard man, quite displeased with tank performance; he was relieving the current tank battalion commander. He undoubtedly worried if I would be an improvement. Ginder was quite affable and he clued me in on what they expected. The tank deadline rate was very high; maintenance was poor. They had had the bad luck of getting caught in a torrential flood when fording a river in their recent move. As usual, there was "no excuse sir." Discipline was also apparently lax. Ginder was a typical hard-nosed infantryman with a good World War II reputation. [158] He suffered the tanks because of the fire support they gave; but they were armored and the doughs had thin shirts with the brunt of the work, particularly in mountainous terrain. We would have to prove ourselves.

It was October 1 when I took command. The battalion executive officer, Maj. Drew Martin (Oklahoma football player and a great soldier), met me the next morning and we drove to the battalion area in his jeep. One company was committed to the front, supporting an infantry regiment in frontline positions. The other two companies were at the battalion area, performing maintenance after a punishing road march in mud, water and foul weather. The luckless former battalion commander was about to leave. He wished me luck and I wondered if I'd be in his shoes in a month or so. I met the staff and the company commanders (except for the one on the front line) and got a quick orientation on the situation. My jeep driver (Higgins) was ready to take me to the forward positions, and we took off. As usual, the enemy had commanding terrain, with a good view of most of the valley road that led to the front line ridge. I could see our smoke pots off to the flank, obscuring an otherwise plainly visible road junction from enemy view. We had been warned about enemy rocket fire on the road ahead, and as we rounded a turn, a couple of rounds landed about 200 yards away near the road. I had Higgins pull in behind a small hill and we waited— trying to time the frequency of incoming. More rounds landed in about a minute. Then nothing for a while, so we took off from the road at full speed, and finally pulled in to our positions under cover. I remember now how quickly I was taken back to Italy; the sound of

---

...*continued*

and retired at the rank of major general. During World War II, Ginder was among the first ashore during the Normandy landings on June 6, 1944.

[158] General Ginder had earned the Distinguished Service Cross for actions on November 28, 1944 during the Battle of Hürtgen Forest.

NOTHING IMPOSSIBLE

incoming rounds again made a familiar quickening of the senses and an excitement which only the combat zone achieves.

I met the company commander and with him had a look at our gun positions—co-located with the infantry sandbagged positions on the line. Barbed wire had been strung, and mines had been laid to the front. Enemy positions were located on a ridge one half a mile or more to our front, but no activity was evident, a normal condition. Normal activity in a defensive position would consist of infantry foot patrols at night, covered by prearranged mortar, artillery, and tank fire (registered previously during the day). In addition, outposts would be manned in no-man's-land on suspected enemy patrol routes, or access routes to our positions. The infantry soldier does this kind of work with noncommissioned officers and/or platoon leaders in charge. And every night patrol brings the chance of encountering an enemy patrol with resultant fire-fight and supporting fires—casualties, prisoners, and the inevitable reports up the chain of command. God bless the infantry. I felt right at home again—checking positions, range cards, equipment, and climbing on tanks. With the tank you want a clean compartment—to include ammunition and weapons; functioning radio and intercom, and clean living quarters—even though sandbagged and dug in. Positions need to be continually improved and even changed if deemed necessary, depending on enemy probing of our suspected locations. In fact, in the next few days I took a fresh look at our positions and changed a few to obtain better fields of fire.

Anyway, General Ruffner had a weekly—Sunday—commander's call, which included regimental and separate unit (i.e. tank) commanders. Here he reviewed the previous activity and laid out general future plans. He was very hard on the regimental commanders—after all they were on a path to become general officers. I'll never forget his introduction to us of Col. Harvey Fischer, [159] commanding the 555th Regimental Combat Team, and just assigned to the division—"now that I've introduced Colonel Fischer, I'll tell you what he did. He allowed an enemy patrol to infiltrate his positions, kill three men, capture four, and take away three machine guns. This will not do at all!" Oh brother, how embarrassing! Poor Fischer was red-faced and so were we. He survived and was later a lieutenant general. You can imagine how we looked forward to those weekly sessions.

---

[159] Harvey H. Fischer (1910-2004) was a California native who graduated from West Point in 1932. He served in the U.S. Army from 1937 to 1967 and retired at the rank of lieutenant general.

My battalion had been charged with constructing a tank firing range to train armored units when they came off the line. This was the IX Corps commander's idea, a very fine and respected armor officer, Lt. Gen. I. D. White. [160] It was he who arranged my going to the 45th Division, rescuing me from the major headquarters in Tokyo. This was a tough job; White expected Fort Knox standards. I organized the effort and had some very fine people to carry out the plan. It was called the Estrada Tank Range—named for a very brave, highly decorated sergeant who had been killed in action a few months previously. It took a few weeks but we were finally ready for the first unit to take the course. General White was on hand, and of course General Ruffner and I were also there to greet him. I had met General Ruffner's helicopter, and got a ride with him to meet the corps commander at the mess tent.

My meeting with the division commander was memorable. He had a deep mistrust of armor formations and armor officers (probably including the corps commander) and of course he had to attend this tank firing event. I think I had earned a modicum of respect, but he had a sardonic way of showing it. "This better be a good tank shoot, Clement" was his greeting as I responded and saluted, "or we'll cut your balls off, won't we driver?" "Yes sir" responded his jeep driver. I burst out laughing and assured him that it would be fine. He had a twinkle in his eyes and we went on to lunch. I had butterflies, wondering how it would go, and almost choked on my food. But it did go well. I was on the back deck of the first tank, with the corps commander. We had head sets and could listen to the crew. The general had some comments, some suggestions for improvement, but on the whole was satisfied. My executive officer, Maj. Drew Martin, had been in charge of getting the range constructed, and used our headquarters company to carry out the plan.

I'll never forget one ceremony held at the tank range. General Ruffner was to present some awards to three or four of my men. But it would be a special formation. He wanted a review—with the division band and one of my companies passing in review—dismounted. Tankers are not foot soldiers nor do they take kindly to marching. I had a company just off the line and in our area for maintenance and reconsti-

---

[160] Isaac D. White (1901-1990) was a New Hampshire native who graduated from Norwich University in 1922. He served in the U.S. Army from 1923 to 1961 and retired at the rank of general. He was a former commandant of the Armor School and was known by colleagues as "Mr. Armor."

tuting from the stint up front. We started a vigorous and accelerated close order drill schedule. I had to fill out the ranks with headquarters troops. The whole thing was quite a challenge but we gave it everything. We had a rehearsal at the tank range; they looked pretty good. At the appointed hour, the division commander and Brig. Gen. P. D. Ginder, his assistant, were on hand. They with me constituted the reviewing stand. The band played the march on; the awards were given; and then the pass in review. I thought they looked good for tankers. We had worked hard. It was then over and we were heading for lunch. General Ruffner said, "I thought it looked pretty good, P. D., how about you?" P. D. then remarked, "They couldn't have done worse if they had marched backwards." I had to laugh—after all of that work. But he was needling me and we had a relaxed lunch.

Dad died in October 1952, but three days had passed before I found out through the Red Cross. He had been buried in Cambridge by then—St. Paul's Cemetery—on 14 Victor Path. I was about to drive up to inspect our front line positions when Father Lubansky, our Catholic chaplain, came up to break the news. He did it quite gently— a nice man. I broke down. Dad was only 65, and it was a complete shock. Heart failure—but he had no history of it. I regrouped and went on with my trip to the front, hoping my driver would not notice my tears. I thought about Mother and how she must be coping. I believe I was able to get a phone call through later and get some of the details. Apparently my late cousin Warren, who lived in Cambridge, took charge. My brothers in California flew in, funeral arrangements were made, and Mother's fortune was decided. She was to fly back to California with Lawrence and live with him. Family members disposed of or acquired the furniture, which was not too much in a three room apartment. I was surprised years later when I saw our fine dining room set, Mother's pride, in Wally Flynn's house in Arlington. I was glad it had a nice home. Wally is my first cousin, once removed; his grandmother was Dad's sister, and his mother, Hazel, was of course my cousin. Lawrence lived in La Canada and Arthur lived not too far away in La Crescenta, in the foothills overlooking Pasadena and Los Angeles. What a champion LaVerne was, Lawrence's wife, taking in my Mother—with three children (Wallace, Laurie, and Joan) it made it a full household. Lawrence later converted his garage into a room for Mother. You could always count on Low in the clutch.

Anyway, back to the war. Early in October, division headquarters held a contingency plan briefing, the plan assuming a forced withdrawal under enemy pressure. Regimental commanders gave their plans, and I, as division armor officer, gave mine. I was happy to use a map colored to show the high ground in the area of operations, putting to good use a technique used at the Command and Staff College. Maneuver in general concerns operating from high ground when possible; "take the high ground" was a common cliché. The session went well. General Ruffner was in charge and asked penetrating questions, like "Clement, what are the tanks going to do?" I explained that the tanks committed to frontline infantry battalions would cover the infantry withdrawal, moving forward or laterally and engaging the enemy on the ridge, withdrawing to prescribed covering positions on high ground to the rear; all of this coordinated with local infantry commanders. I would mount a counterattack with the tank company in reserve at the battalion rear area (in general two of the three tank companies were committed to the front line).

I then pointed out objectives we would aim for in the counterattack up the valley to our front, the whole maneuver designed to buy time for the infantry occupying positions on a rear defensive line. Ruffner liked the counterattack idea, and I think I was invited to the General's Mess for a drink after the briefing. Of course I had gone over the plan with my people, and it was something to check on as we exchanged units on the line, and as people rotated home. Units were in a continual state of flux, replacements taking up slack as high point men went home—combat inexperience exchanged for combat experience, training a never-ending activity.

Captain Ames was my motor officer, and a fine one. He knew his job and had a positive attitude about getting it done. He also had a great sense of humor. You find quickly in the combat zone that you must often be ingenious to get the job done; the book does not teach this. For example, tank spare parts were in short supply, which explained the high dead-line rate when I took over. Ames said he could probably solve most of this if I could turn him loose with a small truck for a few days, amply supplied with our liquor ration. I did, and he did. He came back with parts and contacts for more. Ordnance units in the rear had the parts—but had to follow the requisition system to get them to us—through about five or six different echelons. The barter system worked, and division never asked about how we got our dead-line down; they were smarter than that. If a unit were to write its own operating procedure it would generally depart markedly from "approved" procedure. Standard procedure is written for a common, one-over-the-world doctrine, generally applied. But the individual unit is faced with a particular situation, involving a specific enemy, an environment, and state of readiness. The good unit commander gets the job done, despite the variables. For several more months I continued serving as commander of the 45th Infantry Division's tank battalion, the 245th. This was followed by an assignment as commander of the 3rd Battalion, 279th Infantry of the same division, from April 1953 until after the truce in August 1953.

Following the Korean War, I returned to the U.S. and later Europe for a variety of administrative assignments. First, I did a tour of duty with the Operations Research Office, Johns Hopkins University, which operated under contract with the Department of the Army. Specifically, I served as chief of the Armor Study Group, and then later as advisor to the Operations Division. In fall 1957, I was transferred to the faculty of the U.S. Army War College in Carlisle Barracks, Pennsylvania. I served there as a member of the War Games Group and was later an assistant course director with the Theater Operations Course. I received constructive credit for the War College in June 1958.

In July 1960, I embarked upon an overseas assignment to the U.S. Army Standardization Group [161] in London, England. This brought me back into the research and development program. I served there for a year as deputy and then as commander of the group. Prior to completing this tour, I was able to affect an intra-theater transfer in March 1963. Thus, I took command of the 14th Armored Cavalry Regiment in Fulda, Germany. [162] A highlight of this period was getting to know then-Lt. Gen. Creighton Abrams, a regular visitor to Fulda, who commanded V Corps in Europe from 1963-1964. I would later serve on his staff in Vietnam. Anyways, I remained with the 14th Armored Cavalry until June 1964, when I returned to the United States for duty, again in research and development.

My first assignment of this nature back in the U.S. was as Assistant Director of Army Research, under the Chief of Research and Development at the Pentagon in Washington D.C. In addition, I was commanding officer of the Army Research Office, a research directorate operating under the Director of Army Research. I was nominated for brigadier general rank on 29 November 1965 while occupying this po-

---

[161] The first U.S. Army Material Command (AMC) Research, Development, and Standardization Group came into being at the end of World War II to help sustain the level of interoperability achieved between U.S. and British forces during the war. Other standardization groups were later created with such nations as France, Germany, Canada, and Australia.

[162] Fulda is a city located in the Federal State of Hesse in central Germany.

sition, and was promoted on 1 June 1966. During this period, I also furthered my education and received a master's degree in international relations from George Washington University. From 1966 to 1968, I served with the Deputy Chief of Staff for Personnel, DA, and then as Chief of Staff, Combat Developments Command. However, while these were all constructive assignments, I was eager by this time to get back into the field. I also knew that advancement to major general would require a tour in Vietnam. Thus, I was able to obtain assignment as an assistant division commander with the 23rd Division—also known as the Americal Division—in December 1968. A short time later, I was assigned to MACV [163] as Director of Training for South Vietnamese Army forces on the staff of Gen. Creighton Abrams. A "highlight" of that tour was testifying to Congress on March 3, 1970 about the progress being made on Vietnamization [164]—it was a harrowing experience to be sure. Vietnam—that strange war—it left me with a variety of tales to tell some other time.

I retired from the U.S. Army after 30 years of service on 31 July 1970. I had served overseas for 10 of those years. Following my Army retirement, I worked with various think-tank companies in the Washington D.C. area on military oriented studies before retiring completely to Williamsburg, Virginia in 1985, where I found enjoyment working as an interpreter for the Colonial Williamsburg Foundation. I also stayed active on the veterans' reunion circuit and served as a frequent speaker for the local West Point alumni chapter in Richmond. In addition, I kept busy with family. With my second wife Martha, I had five children—Sarah, Anne, Ellen, David, and Doug. I later remarried and spent retirement with my wife Joan, who has two children: Michael and Cynthia.

I enjoyed every day of my Army career and did my best to keep the faith and uphold my West Point training. My decorations, among others, included the Distinguished Service Cross, the Silver Star, the Bronze Star (for valor), the Legion of Merit (awarded after service in Korea), the Distinguished Service Medal, the Italian Medal for Valor (awarded during World War II when with the 804th Tank Destroyer Battalion), and the South Vietnamese Army Distinguished Service Or-

---

[163] MACV stood for Military Assistance Command, Vietnam.

[164] "Vietnamization" was a policy of the Nixon Administration to expand, equip, and train South Vietnamese military forces and assign them ever-increasing combat roles while steadily reducing the U.S. Military presence in the area.

der (1st Class) for service in Vietnam. I was also proud to have reached general officer rank. I would not have traded it all for the world—it was a good life.

Appendix A

Wallace L. Clement Dates of Rank

Rank	RA	AUS
2nd Lieutenant	11 June 1940	
1st Lieutenant	11 June 1943	11 October 1941
Captain	15 July 1948	29 July 1942
Major	29 August 1952	15 July 1944
Lt. Colonel	11 June 1960	28 December 1950
Colonel	11 June 1965	8 May 1961
Brig. General		1 June 1966

Note: RA (Regular Army) refers to permanent rank while AUS (Army of the United States) refers to temporary rank. During World War II, Korea, and Vietnam, the AUS was the official name for the conscription (i.e. draft) force of the United States Army that was raised at the discretion of Congress when the United States entered a major conflict. At the conclusion of such conflicts, officers who had achieved higher ranks in the AUS were often reverted to their permanent rank in the RA.

Appendix B

Military Decorations of Wallace L. Clement

Distinguished Service Cross
Distinguished Service Medal
Silver Star
Legion of Merit with 2 Oak Leaf Clusters
Distinguished Flying Cross
Bronze Star with Oak Leaf Cluster
Air Medal with 16 Oak Leaf Clusters
Joint Service Commendation Medal
Army Commendation Medal with Oak Leaf Cluster
Army of Occupation Medal—Germany
American Defense Service Medal
American Campaign Medal
European-African-Middle Eastern Campaign Medal
World War II Victory Medal
National Defense Service Medal with Oak Leaf Cluster
Korean Service Medal
Vietnam Service Medal
United Nations Service Medal for Korea
Combat Infantryman Badge
Army Staff Identification Badge
Italian Cross for Military Valor
Vietnamese Cross of Gallantry with Gold Star and Palm
Vietnamese Distinguished Service Order—1st Class

Appendix C

By direction of the President, under the provisions of Army Regulations 600-45, as amended, the Distinguished Service Cross was awarded by the Theater Commander to the officer named below:

WALLACE L. CLEMENT, 023167, Major, Cavalry, for extraordinary heroism against the enemy in the vicinity of Sasso Bolognese, Italy, on 19 April 1945. Accompanying an armored force consisting of one company of tank destroyers and one company of tanks which was assigned the mission of cutting a road behind an enemy force which was blocking the advance of friendly infantry elements, Major Clement, voluntarily taking command, decided to split the armor into two columns and have them converge on the enemy's rear. Despite the fierce battle that was raging around him between the armored elements and the enemy artillery, mortars, machine guns and small arms, he dismounted and went around to all the platoon leaders and most of the tanks and tank destroyers to explain his plan and to give instructions. Returning to his lead vehicle, he ordered an advance and personally led the attack with such determination that the enemy resistance was overrun and the force advanced to the road junctions where the armor was to be split up into two columns. With complete disregard for his personal safety, Major Clement again dismounted, went forward, and supervised the evacuation of the wounded and the removal of the knocked out tank which was then blocking the road. Completing a foot reconnaissance of the left fork of the road under intense fire from snipers and machine gunners, he led his column in an outflanking maneuver and reduced the immediate resistance. The column which he was leading reached its objective that night, outflanking the enemy force and reducing its resistance. Major Clement's heroism, inspiring leadership and indomitable spirit under intense fire exemplify the highest traditions of the Armed Forces of the United States. Entered the United States Military Academy from Massachusetts.

BY COMMAND OF LIEUTENANT GENERAL LEE

L.C. Jaynes

Major General, United States Army

Chief of Staff

26 April 1946

Appendix D

Major Wallace L. Clement, 023167, Cavalry, United States Army. Under the provisions of Army Regulations 600-45, as amended, you are awarded a Bronze Star Medal for heroic achievement in action.

CITATION;

WALLACE L. CLEMENT, Major, Cavalry, United States Army, for heroic achievement in action, on 12 July 1944, near Castiglioncello, Italy. An armored reconnaissance patrol forming for a forced reconnaissance mission was taken under fire by German artillery and mortars. Realizing that the patrol had become ineffective in the face of intense enemy fire, MAJOR CLEMENT (then Captain), left his observation post, moved forward on foot, and under enemy observation and fire, rallied the patrol members. Mounted on the lead vehicle, he led the patrol in a flanking movement, penetrating distance of eight hundred yards within enemy territory. Under his leadership, the patrol routed two enemy outpost positions and inflicted heavy casualties on the opposing force. Major CLEMENT's courageous performance enabled a stronger force to advance one thousand yards without a single serious casualty. Entered the United States Military Academy from Boston, Massachusetts.

Mark W. Clark
Lieutenant General, U.S. Army
Commanding
24 September 1944

Appendix E

U.S. Army MIA Telegram to Mrs. Helen Clement

11 May 1945

Mrs. Helen T. Clement
1218 Massachusetts Avenue
Cambridge, Massachusetts

Dear Mrs. Clement,
This letter is to confirm my recent telegram in which you were regretfully informed that your son, Major Wallace L. Clement, 023167, Cavalry, has been reported missing in action in Italy since 22 April 1945.

I realize the distress caused by failure to receive more information and details; therefore, I wish to assure you that in the event additional information is received at any time, it will be transmitted to you without delay. If no information is received in the meantime, I will communicate with you again three months from the date of this letter.

Inquiries relative to allowances, effects, and allotments should be addressed to the agencies indicated in the enclosed Bulletin of Information.

Permit me to extend to you my heartfelt sympathy during this period of uncertainty.

Sincerely yours,
J.A. Ulio
Major General
The Adjutant General of the Army

Appendix F

804ᵀᴴ Tank Destroyer Battalion
List of Enemy Equipment Destroyed

Company A

No.	Item	Date
1	Artillery Piece	28 April 1944
1	Tank (unknown type)	13 May 1944
9	Machine Gun Nests	13 May 1944
2	Vehicles	6 June 1944
3	Machine Gun Nests	27 June 1944
2	Anti-Tank Guns (75mm)	27 June 1944
1	Tank (unknown type)	28 June 1944
1	Armored Vehicle	1 July 1944
2	Anti-Tank Guns	5 July 1944
2	Machine Gun Nests	14 July 1944
2	Bazooka Crews	14 July 1944
3	Cargo Trucks	18 July 1944
2	Machine Gun Nests	14 September 1944
3	Mortars	14 September 1944
1	Vehicle	14 September 1944
2	Machine Gun Nests	8 October 1944
2	Mortars	13 October 1944
1	Supply Point	16 October 1944
1	Anti-Tank Gun	16 October 1944
1	Cargo Truck	16 October 1944
3	Machine Gun Nests	18 October 1944
1	Supply Point	20 October 1944
1	Tank (unknown type)	21 October 1944
	Ammo Dump Set on Fire	
1	Mortar	1 November 1944
	Ammo Dump Set on Fire	

6	Pill Boxes	17 April 1945
5	Horse Drawn Carts (supplies and troops)	24 April 1945
1	Scout Car	24 April 1945
2	Motorcycles	24 April 1945
1	Jeep	24 April 1945
3	Half Tracks	24 April 1945
2	Field Guns (75mm)	24 April 1945
1	Horse Drawn Ammo Wagon	24 April 1945
2	Horse Drawn Carts (supplies and troops)	25 April 1945
1	Cargo Truck	25 April 1945
2	Cargo Trucks	28 April 1945
2	Anti-Tank Guns	29 April 1945
2	Bazooka Crews	29 April 1945
10	Trucks and Horse Drawn Carts	30 April 1945
15	Cargo Trucks	1 May 1945
1	Anti-Tank Gun	1 May 1945
2	Bazooka Crews	1 May 1945
2	Armored Cars	1 May 1945
1	Half Track	1 May 1945
2	Motorcycles	1 May 1945
1	Anti-Aircraft Gun (20mm)	1 May 1945
4	Machine Gun Nests	1 May 1945
1	Half Track	2 May 1945
1	Amphibious Jeep	2 May 1945

Company B

No.	Item	Date
1	Field Gun	27 March 1944
1	Field Gun (type unknown)	3 April 1944
2	Anti-Tank Guns	7 June 1944
2	Tanks (type unknown)	7 June 1944
1	Tank (type unknown)	9 July 1944
1	Field Gun (type unknown)	10 July 1944
1	Field Gun	16 September 1944
1	Half Track (personnel carrier)	27 September 1944
1	Vehicle	8 October 1944
3	Mortars	8 October 1944
1	Cargo Truck	15 November 1944
1	Vehicle	5 January 1945
1	Pill Box	18 April 1945
1	Field Gun	21 April 1945

7	Vehicles	23 April 1945
2	Anti-Tank Guns	23 April 1945
1	Tank (type unknown)	25 April 1945
1	Field Gun	25 April 1945
1	Machine Gun Nest	26 April 1945
1	Machine Gun	27 April 1945
1	Anti-Tank Gun	27 April 1945
6	Staff Vehicles	27 April 1945
2	Bazookas	27 April 1945
1	Field Gun	29 April 1945
5	Cargo Trucks	29 April 1945
2	Personnel Carriers	29 April 1945
4	Staff Vehicles	30 April 1945
1	Mortar	30 April 1945
6	Horse Drawn Carts	30 April 1945
1	Machine Gun Nest	30 April 1945
8	Small Trucks	30 April 1945
2	Jeeps	30 April 1945
1	Motorcycle	30 April 1945
6	Cargo Trucks	1 May 1945
8	Horse Drawn Carts (supplies and troops)	1 May 1945

Company C

No.	Item	Date
9	Machine Gun Nests	12 May 1944
1	Tank (MK 4)	12 May 1944
2	Mortars	12 May 1944
2	Cargo Trucks	5 June 1944
1	Tank (type unknown)	9 June 1944
6	Machine Gun Nests	26 June 1944
1	Tank (type unknown)	27 June 1944
2	Machine Gun Nests	27 June 1944
1	Mortar	28 June 1944
1	Jeep	28 June 1944
1	Cargo Truck	29 June 1944
1	Anti-Aircraft Gun (20mm)	29 June 1944
1	Machine Gun Nest	29 June 1944
1	Tank (type unknown)	30 June 1944
4	Anti-Tank Guns	1 July 1944
3	Tanks (MK 4)	1 July 1944
4	Mortars	2 July 1944

1	Cargo Truck	2 July 1944
1	Anti-Aircraft Gun (20mm)	2 July 1944
2	Machine Gun Nests	11 July 1944
1	Anti-Tank Gun (88mm)	11 July 1944
1	Tank (type unknown)	18 July 1944
3	Machine Gun Nests	18 July 1944
1	Anti-Tank Gun	18 July 1944
1	Vehicle	19 July 1944
7	Machine Gun Nests	13 September 1944
1	Anti-Tank Gun (75mm)	13 September 1944
1	Anti-Tank Gun (caliber unknown)	26 September 1944
1	Anti-Tank Gun (caliber unknown)	27 September 1944
2	Tanks (type unknown)	27 September 1944
9	Machine Gun Nests	17 October 1944
7	Machine Gun Nests	18 October 1944
1	Tank (type unknown)	27 September 1944
1	Vehicle	9 March 1945
2	Machine Gun Nests	17 April 1945
3	Machine Gun Nests	17 April 1945
1	Mortar	17 April 1945
2	Machine Gun Nests	18 April 1945
6	Machine Gun Nests	20 April 1945
2	Bazookas	20 April 1945
1	Anti-Tank Gun (caliber unknown)	20 April 1945
1	Tank (MK 4)	21 April 1945
1	Tank (MK 3)	21 April 1945
1	Machine Gun Nest	21 April 1945
3	Cargo Trucks	21 April 1945
1	Anti-Tank Gun (20 mm)	21 April 1945
1	Anti-Tank Gun (caliber unknown)	22 April 1945
1	Machine Gun Nest	22 April 1945
1	Tank (MK 5)	24 April 1945
1	Tank (MK 4)	24 April 1945
1	Field Gun	24 April 1945
1	Anti-Tank Gun (caliber unknown)	24 April 1945
4	Machine Gun Nests	24 April 1945
5	Cargo Trucks	28 April 1945
12	Horse Driven Carts	29 April 1945
17	Horse Driven Carts (supplies and ammo)	30 April 1945
1	Snow Plow	3 May 1945

Reconnaissance Company

No.	Item	Date
2	Mortars (120 mm)	2 July 1944
1	Mortar (81 mm)	14 July 1944
1	Cargo Truck	24 March 1945

804TH TANK DESTROYER BATTALION
LIST OF ENEMY PERSONNEL CAPTURED

Company A

No.	Item	Date
185	Officers and Men	23 April 1945
162	Officers and Men	24 April 1945
150	Officers and Men	26 April 1945
475	Officers and Men	28 April 1945
200	Officers, Nurses, and Men (Hospital)	28 April 1945
628	Officers and Men	29 April 1945
300	Officers, Nurses, and Men (Hospital)	29 April 1945
3	Officers	30 April 1945
Assisted in capture of 5,000 Officers and Men		2 May 1945

Company B

No.	Item	Date
70	Officers and Men	26 April 1945
280	Officers and Men	29 April 1945
1200	Officers and Men	30 April 1945

Company C

No.	Item	Date
26	Officers and Men	17 April 1945
40	Officers and Men	20 April 1945
19	Enlisted Men	21 April 1945
36	Enlisted Men	22 April 1945
131	Officers and Men	24 April 1945
200	Officers and Men	28 April 1945
185	Officers and Men	29 April 1945
156	Officers and Men	30 April 1945
176	Officers and Men	2 May 1945
201	Officers and Men	3 May 1945
50	Officers and Men	4 May 1945

Reconnaissance Company

No.	Item	Date
15	Officers and Men	2 July 1944
1844	Officers and Men	16 April-2 May 1945

NOTHING IMPOSSIBLE

Appendix G

LETTER FROM 804TH TDB VETERAN MORRIS H. SNOW
TO COL. DAVID CLEMENT (USMCR, RET.)

July 16, 2001

Dear David,

I find it takes me longer each year to get cranked up to do something. Have you heard from Shorty Moore (1st Lt. Byrel A. Moore) or Clarence Troeger? Their wives are experiencing some health problems. Lois Troeger is having some carpal tunnel problems and is experiencing quite some pain. Shorty's wife had had some problems for quite some time. She has fallen quite recently, probably four months ago and spent some time in the hospital and nursing homes. Shorty has her at home now and she is doing some better. He is doing a terrific job taking care of her. Audrey and I are doing reasonably well. Our kids were here for July 4th. One family from California and the other from Kansas. We had a great time and the kids had a lot of fun together. They took a trip to Carlsbad Caverns—the Kansas kids had not been there before and were quite favorably impressed. Enough of that.

Here are some memories I have of your Dad. All of them favorable, I have no unfavorable memories. He did get on me one time. This was in Africa, I was a platoon sergeant, and one of my men had gone AWOL for a day or two, or was late coming in from Pass. Anyway, he called us into his tent and chewed us out. Me for not having control of my men, and my man for being late. He took us outside and pointed out a prominent bush about half a mile down the road, and said, "Sergeant Snow, I want this man to double time down to that bush and back, every morning, and I want you to see that he does it. I said "Yes, Sir—I will stand here and watch." He said, "No, you go with him and I'll stand here and watch." Your Dad's timing was terrific—we made one trip, and moved out that afternoon. I didn't have as close of relations with your Dad as Shorty and Troeger. They both served as first sergeant. Shorty was first sergeant from about September 1943 until August 1944. When Shorty was away for any reason, Troeger served as 1SG.

Clarence Troeger received a battlefield commission in about August 1944. I think he might have been the first one in the battalion to receive a commission. Shorty received one about a month later. In September 1944, I was wounded and spent a couple of months in the hospital. When I returned to duty, I was given a little time to see if I could get used to the noises again. One or two of the men were just so shook up, they could not get used to the shelling and weren't able to stay. Anyways, upon my return I heard an amusing story about our lieutenant. This lieutenant called for his jeep one day and the driver took him to Florence as ordered. After waiting a couple of hours for the lieutenant, the driver decided on his own initiative that he and the jeep may be needed back at the platoon. He left the lieutenant a small note and drove away. Your Dad later ran into the lieutenant in Naples and had a visit. However, your Dad reported that nothing was said about the driver leaving.

Now I will back up to the first meeting with your Dad. We were in La Mesa, California (about April 1942). The battalion had a change of organization and a "Recon" company was organized. Fred Rowell was "A" Company commander and he went with the cadre as C.O. for the new reconnaissance company. Your Dad came to the 804th as "A" Company C.O. He came from a horse cavalry unit on the Mexican border. The first time we saw him, he had on his riding clothes with a broad-brimmed hat. We kind of wondered just what we had there, and later I found out that he wondered what he was going to do with that band of sheep herders, cowboys, pipeline builders, soda jerks and grocery clerks. It all worked out real well. The transition was real smooth—I held him quite in awe, and always did.

We moved to Fort Hood in April/May of 1942, and a tank destroyer OCS had been established. A lot of the men—particularly platoon sergeants and first sergeants—went to OCS. Shorty Moore, Robert Brown, and I were made platoon sergeants around that time. Farris Jeffreys was our new first sergeant. We had all been buck sergeants until that time. We received some men from a TD battalion that was being re-adjusted or being disbanded or something—they were good men. We trained from some time at Fort Hood, which at that time was merely a designated area as they were building the permanent location. After about three months there, we received orders to report to Indiantown Gap, Pennsylvania—preparatory to embarking to Ireland, then to England and Africa. The battalion was not committed to action, but our equipment was taken as replacements to units in combat. After some training in Africa, we were assigned to escort German prisoners to England, then on to the U.S. When we reported to Camp Patrick Henry, Virginia to go back to Africa, we had physicals. First Sergeant Jeffrey had ulcers and didn't go back with us. Shorty Moore became first sergeant and Troeger was platoon sergeant. One of the memorable experiences in Africa was the gazelle hunts. We were hunting for camp meat. This was after the war had ended in that area and we had to feed German prisoners. That put us on pretty short rations. Don't remember if your Dad went on one of those or not. Jim Webster was in charge of the group that I was in.

Anyways, I was on an advance detail to go to Italy in January 1944. I was attached to a tank destroyer battalion in the Casino area to get some combat experience and see how their units operated. I spent four or five weeks with them, then rejoined the battalion when they came over. One of my first assignments after we went on line was when your Dad assigned me and Bill Page to operate an artillery outpost overlooking Castelforte. We were there about two weeks and were then relieved by division artillery. Later on, your Dad called for me one day to report to Company HQ. Eber Peters had been my platoon leader and he went to CO HQ as executive officer and was promoted to first lieutenant. When I reported in, your Dad said, "Meet Lieutenant Lyle. He is your new platoon leader." This lieutenant was the screwiest, bleary-eyed thing I had ever seen. He was lying on a couple of barracks bags, unshaven, and red faced. Lieutenant Lyle spent a lot of time in the hospital and off duty. I learned a lot of this after your Dad started coming to the reunions.

Later on we started the preparation to go to Rome. My platoon dug emplacements for our tank destroyers and the night of the attack, we went into our position under the noise of the artillery barrage. We started firing on designated targets across the valley. Your Dad came by to check on us and climbed up on each TD to see how we were doing. One of the men then said, "Captain, you'd better get down or you are going to get hit!" Your Dad responded, "This is what I've trained for all my life." He was real gutsy and also very thorough. Just before we crossed the Arno River, your Dad was assigned to Battalion HQ and promoted to major. Before we started the drive to Rome, Colonel Purdy went to the hospital and didn't come back. Back at Camp Hood, Fred Rowell had also been assigned to battalion staff and promoted to major. C.M. Woodbury had also been on battalion staff as a major. Later, an M4 tank battalion needed a battalion commander, and that was an opportunity for Woodbury and he took it. I'm telling you all of this to tell you that all three of these men became brigadier generals, and all of them came through "A" Company. Many years later, your Dad and I were talking on the phone one day and he said, "You know we had a good outfit, didn't we?" I answered and told him that he had done a good job and had raised five battlefield-commissioned second lieutenants, and he said, "That's right." I then said that those lieutenants didn't do too bad either, and that our battalion had also raised three brigadier generals. Your Dad kind of got a kick out of that!

In about 1983-1984, John Gaddy, who was secretary and treasurer of our group, called me and said, "I have found an address on Wallace Clement." I said, "That's great! Write and tell him about the reunion." Gaddy—who had been a corporal during the war, responded, "I don't know... he's a brigadier general." I then told him to just give me the address and I would track down a phone number and call him myself. I called your Dad and he was quite surprised to hear from me. I told him about the reunion and he said, "I don't know whether anyone wants to see me." I told him to come on and that he would be treated like a king. We talked on the phone several times, and one time he said, "I'm going to California to see my sons and when I come back through Albuquerque, if timing and everything is right I'll call you." He called one afternoon and asked if it would be OK to come to Roswell the next morning. I told him to call when he got to town. He called the next morning and said he had checked in at the motel. I said, "Tell me what time and I will pick you up and we'll go eat." We picked him up about 5:30pm, and went to eat at a steak house. After dinner we came back to our house. I'll back track here a little. When we bought this house it had a two-car, carport. We closed that in and installed an overhead door. Audrey gave me instructions that there could be no shelves, no work bench, or anything like that—just cars. And that's the way it is. Anyway, when we pulled in the driveway and opened the garage door, your Dad said, "You must be very poor—you can get your car in the garage!" That is some of your Dad's wit.

John and Lou Gaddy came over and we had a real good visit. I took your Dad back over to the motel about 10:30pm. John Gaddy was afraid your Dad would not want to see him. During the war, your Dad had busted him from sergeant one time and John took it personal. Several of the other men made similar remarks like John, saying "He won't want to see me—I caused him too much trouble." However, after your Dad came to the reunion and the men got to visit with him, all of the anxiety was gone. For all of those years after the war, your Dad was no longer responsible to us or for us. We could all just be friends. Nevertheless, the men were still a bit awed in his presence—after all, your Dad was a brigadier general. One of the men said, "You know, considering all the things I did he treated me real good." One example—when we were at Camp Hood, we went to some of the little towns and did a parade, and spent the night. Our company went to Belton, Texas. The guy I was just writing about got drunk and rode into town astride the back of a 75 mm gun. Your Dad put him in the brig, which was a ¾-ton truck with the canvas pulled down on it. The guy said that he never got so hot in his life. On this same trip, one of the men, while we were in California, got a half track and took his girlfriend home to Brawley in it. On the way back, he was running low on gas and pulled into a service station and said "Filler up!" When the attendant had filled the tank and checked the oil, the guy told him, "Charge it to Uncle Sam," and then drove off. The California Highway Patrol picked him up shortly after that. I don't remember what kind of punishment he got for that, but not much—probably forfeiture of some pay and confinement.

Anyway, the night we spent in Belton was on the courthouse lawn. The man I just wrote about told the lieutenant (a bunch of officers were around the kitchen truck eating dinner) that he had screwed up a lot in this Army but was going to start soldiering and make the best soldier in the outfit. The next morning at roll call, he wasn't there. Nobody saw him leave or act like he was leaving. The last anyone saw of him, he was talking to some girls in a car. He didn't show up and in a reasonable length of time, your Dad started to send someone to West Virginia (where I believe he was from) to see if they could find him. However, your Dad then had second thoughts and said, "I'd better not do that—they may actually find him!" So he left it well enough alone. We really had some dingers in our outfit and some real good soldiers. When things got serious, everyone squared around. All of the men are real proud of your Dad—he was so congenial and ready to talk. He was our speaker at several reunions and the men appreciated him for that.

I'm sending some newsletters and pictures with information on back. I will also be sending reunion notices in a week or so and will send you and your Mother one—and everyone is invited. The biggest reunion we ever had was at the 40th anniversary of the end of the war in 1985. Last year we had 20 men and 35 wives, children, and grand-children for a total of 55. We have lost several men this year. Hope you can read this OK. I'll close.

God Bless,

Morris H. Snow
2nd *Lieutenant*, 804th Tank Destroyer Battalion

Appendix H

SOME HIGHLIGHTS OF THE
804TH TANK DESTROYER BATTALION IN EUROPE

- The English, so hospitable at Christmas time, trying to make the Yanks feel at home.

- The Irish girls with their sturdy legs, able to dance for hours and then walk for miles.

- Drill call in Ireland—dark and wet.

- The practice alert and march from Crom Castle to Newtown Butler and back.

- The range and hike back from it to Crom.

- The long train ride to Belfast on pass.

- London.

- Arabs peddling oranges and eggs, with prices skyrocketing immediately.

- The Battle of El Gor.

- The beach at Beni-Saf.

- Four miles in forty-two minutes.

- General Wilbur's School.

- The moving target range at Sebdou with the imperturbable Arabs refusing to move out of the impact area.

- Winter at Sebdou with the Arabs seemingly closing in on us—and the one who was hit with a red flare by an industrious C Company guard.

- That tasty gazelle meat.

- May 11, 1944—what a show that was when the whole Allied line started to move.

- The Goums—colorful, excitable, and terrifying to the Krauts.

- Newly liberated Italian towns, with cheering people throwing flowers, kisses and waving wine bottles.

- Triumphal entry into Rome.

- Living off the land, each tank laden with vegetables, eggs, and even chickens, and each crew having at least one good cook.

- Rest camps in Florence and Rome.

- Rotation—always stunning news.

- Mt. Adone.

- Breaking into the Po Valley after all those months.

- Krauts withdrawing—and the Kraut convoy passing at night with neither force aware of the other.

- The Alps—beautiful but not nice for fighting.

- Cessation of hostilities, with Krauts and Yanks patrolling the same streets, both armed.

- The various kinds of beverage in various parts of the world—port, stout, vin blanc, muscatel, cognac, vino bianco, etc.

- Montecatini, preparing to go to Japan via the States.

- The *Marine Raven*—"Keep the ship clean"—and a "Special good morning to the cooks and KP's."

- Civilians again, after all these years.

FINITO

804th Tank Destroyer Battalion

Unit History

Converted in January, 1942, from the 104th Infantry Antitank Battalion, 45th Infantry Division, at Camp San Luis Obispo, California. Arrived Belfast, Ireland, on 17 August, 1942, and at Oran, Algeria, on 1 February, 1943. Trained French troops on M10s in North Africa; only battalion observers went to front. Arrived at Naples, Italy, on 8 February, 1944, and moved to Gustav Line along Garigliano River by 9 March. Entered Rome on 4 June. Carried doughs into Livorno on 18 July. Crossed Arno River in September, then supported attack on Gothic Line through October. Broke into Po River Valley in April 1945, crossed Po River on 27 April. Company C was part of column that linked up with U.S. Seventh Army troops in Brenner Pass on 5 May.

Attached To

34th, 85th, 88th, 91st Infantry divisions.

Combat Equipment

March 1944 – M10

Commanding Officers

Lt. Col. Edward Purdy, original CO – January 1941)
Lt. Col. Fred G. Rowell – March 1944

Code Names

Unknown

Campaign Credits

Rome Arno – January 22 to September 9, 1944
North Apennines – September 10, 1944 to April 4, 1945
Po Valley – April 5 to May 8, 1945

Awards

Croix De Guerre (French or Belgium "Cross of War")

Location August 1945

Camp Hood, Texas

Bibliography

Brooks, Thomas R. *The War North of Rome: June 1944-May 1945*. Edison, NJ: Castle Books, 1996.

Clement, Wallace L., ed. *804ᵗʰ Tank Destroyer Battalion, 1941-1945: A History*. Camp Hood, TX: U.S. Army, 1945.

Henderson, G.F.R. *Stonewall Jackson and the American Civil War*. New York: Da Capo Press, 1988.

Howe, George F., ed. *19 Days from the Apennines to the Alps: The Story of the Po Valley Campaign*. Washington, D.C.: U.S. Fifth Army, 1945.

Jomini, Antoine H. *Life of Napoleon*. New York: HardPress Publishing, 2013.

Steele, Matthew F. *American Campaigns*. London: Forgotten Books Publishing, 2015.

Sulzberger, C.L. *The American Heritage Picture History of World War II*. New York: American Heritage Publishers, 1966.

Van Wagenen, Jean. *The Road Back*. Los Angeles: Jean Van Wagenen, 1988.

Westwell, Ian. *World War II Commanders: From the Attack on Poland to the Surrender of Japan*. New York: Metro Books, 2008.

Arthur Clement (Clement Family Collection).

Harry E. Widener Library, Harvard University, Cambridge, Massachusetts (Library of Congress).

Helen Murphy Clement (Clement Family Collection).

West Point Cadet Wallace L. Clement (Clement Family Collection).

The West Point Boxing Team, March 1939. Cadet Wallace L. Clement is shown on the back row, standing third from left (Clement Family Collection).

The West Point Baseball Team, May 1940. Cadet Wallace L. Clement is shown on the front row, seated third from left (Clement Family Collection).

Lt. Wallace L. Clement, U.S. Cavalry, June 1940 (Clement Family Collection).

E Troop, 11th U.S. Cavalry at the Del Mar Race Track during the San Diego County Fair, April 1941. Lt. Wallace L. Clement, platoon leader for the machine gun platoon, is shown on the left (Clement Family Collection).

Desert training in Texas with an M3 Gun Motor Carriage tank destroyer, Summer 1942 (U.S. Army Photograph).

Built in 1820, Crom Castle is located on the shores of the Upper Lough Erne in County Fermanagh, Northern Ireland. The castle is privately owned by the Crichton family, Earls of Erne, but was made available to the U.S. Army for training purposes during World War II (U.S. Army Photograph).

Maj. Gen. George S. Patton affixing the Medal of Honor upon Brig. Gen. William H. Wilbur in the presence of Gen. George C. Marshall and Pres. Franklin D. Roosevelt, January 1943 (Library of Congress).

Field Marshall Erwin Rommel, commander of German and Italian forces in North Africa from 1941 to 1943 (Collection of the Editor).

Sgt. Reed Van Wagenen, August 1943 (Clement Family Collection).

Capt. Wallace L. Clement on the beach at Beni Saf in northwestern Algeria, 1943 (Clement Family Collection).

NOTHING IMPOSSIBLE

Lt. Col. Fred Rowell, Summer 1944 (U.S. Army Photograph).

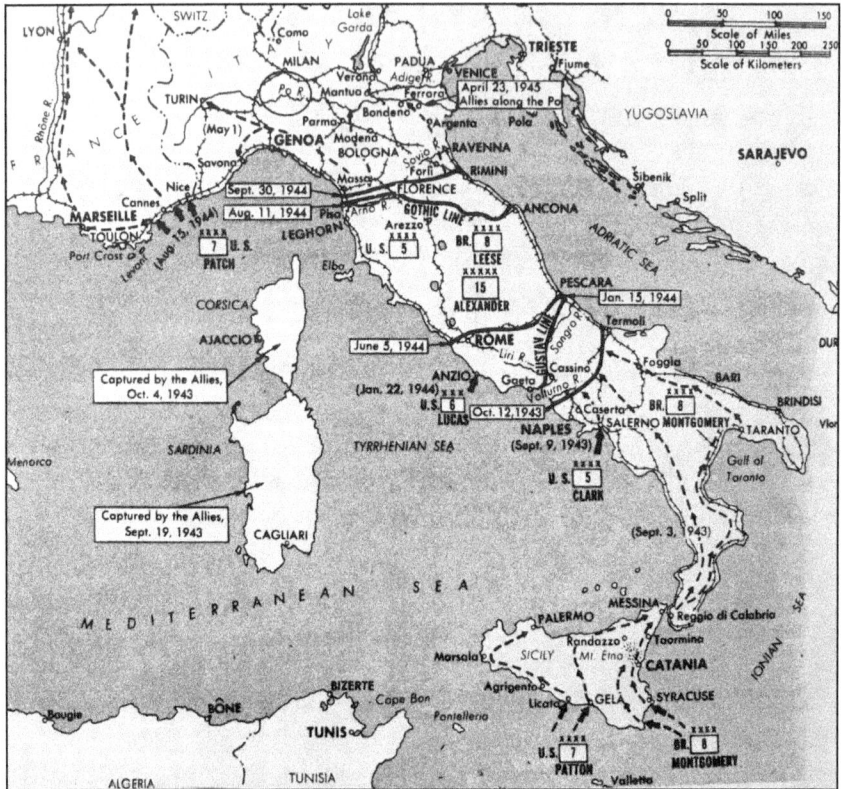

This campaign map displays the progress that Allied Forces made in Italy during the later stages of World War II. The 804th Tank Destroyer Battalion was among these forces that fought the length of Italy's "boot" (Clement Family Collection).

NOTHING IMPOSSIBLE

Lt. Gen. Lucian Truscott, Fall 1944 (Library of Congress).

Monghidoro following direct firing from the 804th Tank Destroyer Battalion's B Company, October 1944 (U.S. Army Photograph).

German dead lay on the streets in this unidentified Italian town as the tide of battle rolls on, Spring 1945 (U.S. Army Photograph).

Long columns of enemy prisoners became a common sight for the Allies as the German war effort in Italy began to collapse, Spring 1945 (U.S. Army Photograph).

Nazi SS Obergruppenführer Karl Wolff, Supreme Commander of all SS forces in Italy. The rank of obergruppenführer was equivalent to the rank of lieutenant general in the American and British Armies (Collection of the Editor).

Major Wallace L. Clement (second from left) conferring with colleagues following his release as a POW – May 1945 (Clement Family Collection).

804th Tank Destroyer Battalion personnel returning home to the United States on board the SS Marine Raven – July 1945 (U.S. Army Photograph).

Officers of the 804th Tank Destroyer Battalion in Feltre, Italy – May 1945. Major Wallace L. Clement is seated on the front row, fourth from the right (Clement Family Collection).

Major Wallace L. Clement (right) with his brother, Lt. Lawrence Clement, on postwar occupation duty in Germany in 1946 (Photo Courtesy of Wally Clement).

Lt. Col. Wallace L. Clement, commanding officer of the 245th Tank Battalion, seated in his office on the front in Korea – October 1952 (Clement Family Collection).

Lt. Gen. Ira D. White and Maj. Gen. David L. Ruffner inspect a tank crew of the 245th Tank Battalion, 45th Infantry Division, at the dedication ceremony for the Estrada Tank Range on 16 November 1952. Lt. Col. Wallace L. Clement is on the far right (U.S. Army Photograph).

Lt. Gen. Ira D. White inspects the Honor Guard of the 245th Tank Battalion, 45th Infantry Division, at the dedication ceremony for the Estrada Tank Range on 16 November 1952. The rest of the inspection party consisted of (from left to right): Brig. Gen. P. D. Ginder, Maj. Gen. David L. Ruffner, Lt. Col. Wallace L. Clement, and Lt. David C. Koch (U.S. Army Photograph).

Capt. Victor Moore (shown on right) is congratulated by Lt. Col. Wallace L. Clement after receiving the Bronze Star Medal for Meritorious Service. The presentation took place at the 245th Tank Battalion Headquarters on 20 November 1952 north of Inje, Korea (U.S. Army Photograph).

Maj. Gen. H.G. Sparrow and Mrs. Martha Clement pin stars on newly promoted Brig. Gen. Wallace L. Clement – June 1966 (U.S. Army Photograph).

Rex L. Burns on left and an unknown soldier on right of the 804th Tank Destroyer Battalion pose with their M1 Submachine Guns. The photo was taken while the unit was stationed in Belfast, Ireland in August of 1942.

Officers and men of the 804th Tank Destroyer Battalion outside Crom Castle.

NOTHING IMPOSSIBLE

Jeeps and M8 Armored Car from the 804th Tank Destroyer Battalion (supporting the 88th Division), Gaeta, Italy, 20 May 1944.

M10 from the 804ᵗʰ Tank Destroyer Battalion firing as indirect artillery support.

M10 Gun Motor Carriage of the 804ᵗʰ Tank Destroyer Battalion. Looks like a make-shift camp with a tarp over the front hatches and a tent, out of view, to the right.

A group of soldiers from Company A, 804ᵗʰ Tank Destroyer Battalion, taken in the Alps just after the German surrender. Shown in front left to right, Romanick, Smyth, Squible, Alphonso, J. Pangonis and John McKillen. Middle row left to right, Hale, Eldon Pittman, John T. Gaddy, R. Thompson, Samuel W. DeStephano, Thompson, LaMonde, Joe Kinnich and an unknown soldier. On top of the tank destroyer left to right, Bill Martin, Louis George, Joe Romeco and Ted Martin.

Photo of an unknown soldier that was found in the possessions of a member of the 804ᵗʰ Tank Destroyer Battalion, so it is believed this soldier was also part of the 804ᵗʰ. Note that he is wearing the same Fifth Army patch as the other men of the unit wore.

M10 Gun Motor Carriage (GMC) tank destroyer.

NOTHING IMPOSSIBLE

M10 GMC with a panther painted on the rear of the turret weights.

Tank Destroyer Panther shoulder patch. Early eight wheel version.

Tank Destroyer Panther shoulder patch. Later four wheel version.

Nothing Impossible

"This Is Camp Hood" brochure cover. Describes itself as a Camera Trip Through the Army's Tank Destroyer Center. Approximately 14 two-sided pages plus the cover. Undated.

Small 11-page booklet actually put out by the Southwestern Bell Telephone Company who handled the phone service on the base. The back of the book has two pages for names and phone numbers as well as a phone rates chart when calling from Camp Hood.

NOTHING IMPOSSIBLE

Main Entrance, Camp Hood, Texas, the Home of the Tank Destroyers.

Headquarters of the Tank Destroyer Center in Camp Hood, Texas. There is a film crew and a band in the image. There may have been high-ranking officers or dignitaries there for the day. Could possibly have been opening day for the new facility.

Wedding at chapel, Camp Hood, Texas.

One of the Tank Destroyer Bands, Camp Hood, Texas.

Close Combat Fire developed by the Tank Destroyers, Camp Hood, Texas.

A Company of M3 Gun Motor Carriage tank destroyers in line at Camp Hood, Texas.

Company of Tank Destroyer WACS at Camp Hood, Texas.

Dismounted review of soldiers, Camp Hood, Texas.

M3 GMC tank destroyer and crew, Camp Hood, Texas.

Inside view of M3 GMC tank destroyer gun crew in action, Camp Hood, Texas.

NOTHING IMPOSSIBLE

Mounted review of M3 GMC tank destroyers, Camp Hood, Texas.

Portion of Nazi village at Camp Hood, Texas, used in teaching village fighting.

Live machine gun firing provides realism in tank destroyer training at Camp Hood, Texas.

Rope climbing on the tank destroyer obstacle course, Camp Hood, Texas.

M3 GMC tank destroyer during training at Camp Hood, Texas.

Water hazard, tank destroyer obstacle course, Camp Hood, Texas.

M3 GMC tank destroyer with crew.

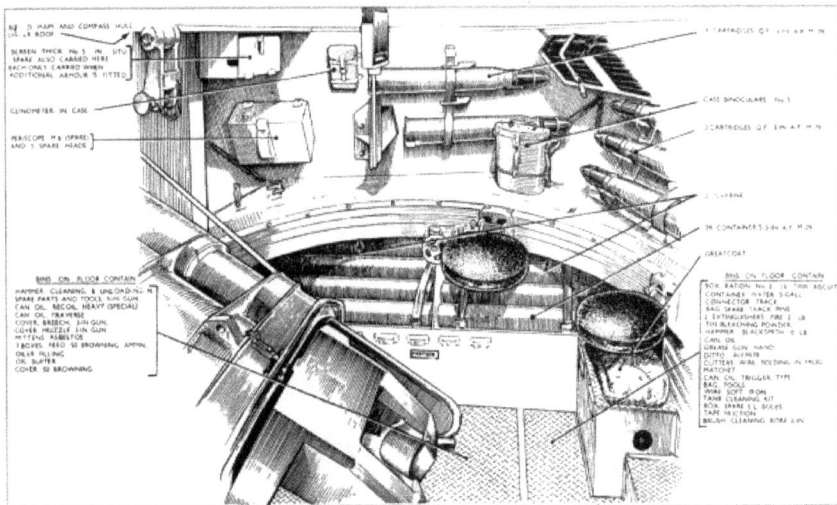

Interior view of right side of the M3 GMC tank destroyer.

NOTHING IMPOSSIBLE

Patch worn by intsructors at the Tank Destroyer School, Camp Hood, Texas.

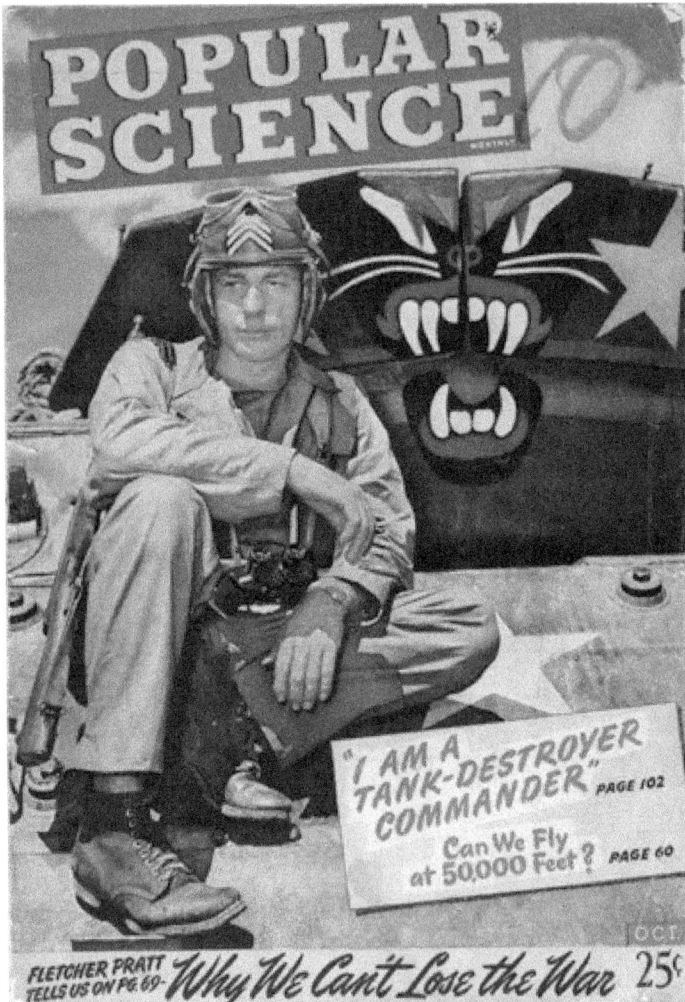

Cover of the October 1943 issue of Popular Science magazine. Five page article within, "I Am A Tank-Destroyer Commander" describes the life of Sergeant Thurman Horton of Clarkton, North Carolina, and his crew in their hard-hitting M10 GMC "Panther."

NOTHING IMPOSSIBLE